LIVING LIFE AS IT C

LIVING LIFE AS IT COMES

POST-DISASTER REFLECTIONS OF A ZEN PRIEST IN FUKUSHIMA

GEN'YŪ SŌKYŪ

Japan Publishing Industry Foundation for Culture

Notes to the Reader:

This book follows the Hepburn system of romanization, with long vowels indicated by macrons. Names are given in the customary Japanese order, surname first.

Living Life as It Comes: Post-Disaster Reflections of a Zen Priest in Fukushima
Gen'yū Sōkyū.

Published by
Japan Publishing Industry Foundation for Culture (JPIC)
2-2-30 Kanda-Jinbocho, Chiyoda-ku, Tokyo 101-0051, Japan

First English edition
Ebook: March 2022
Hardcover: June 2022

Originally published in Japanese under the title *Nariyuki o ikiru: "Ui no okuyama" tsuzuraore* by Chikumashobo Ltd. in 2020.
English publishing rights arranged with Chikumashobo Ltd.

The Japan Publishing Industry Foundation for Culture wishes to express its deep appreciation to Emeritus Professor Patricia Fister of the International Research Center for Japanese Studies for her generous cooperation and guidance in the production of this book.

Jacket and cover design: alema Co., Ltd.

Printed in Japan
ISBN 978-4-86658-218-4
https://www.jpic.or.jp/

Contents

Preface to the English Edition		9
Preface: Living Life as It Comes		12

1. We Are All the Same Age — 16
2. Soaring through Inconvenience — 19
3. Flowers for the Buddha — 21
4. The Tenacity of Five-Storied Pagodas and Prayers — 24
5. Best of Health to Your Ancestors, Too — 27
6. Human Rights — 30
7. Taboo Words — 33
8. *Colds and Their Benefits* — 36
9. *The Chrysanthemum and the Sword* and Duality — 39
10. The Boat on the Hill — 42
11. Efficiency and Harmony — 45
12. Campbell-sensei — 48
13. A Country in Need of Constant Tending — 50
14. Snake Eyes — 53

15.	Equinoxes and Obon	56
16.	Decaying Homes	59
17.	The Price of Economizing	62
18.	The Feeling of Freshness	65
19.	Solicitations	68
20.	The Eight Winds	71
21.	Chestnut Flowers	74
22.	Publishing Academic Papers	77
23.	The New "Dream Island" Concept	80
24.	The "Fukushima 50"	83
25.	The Virtue of Forgetting	86
26.	Symbiosis	89
27.	Okinawan Graves	92
28.	Soft Stone?	95
29.	One-*mon* Prayers	98
30.	Carpenter Bees vs. Carpenters	101
31.	Kawauchi and Rhododendrons	104
32.	The Power of Resolve	107
33.	The Linear Precipitation Zone	109
34.	The Nanto Rinzankai	112
35.	Losing Is Winning	115
36.	*Myōhō*	117
37.	Big Data	120
38.	*Asa* (Morning)	123
39.	Resilience and *Kotobuki*	126
40.	Faint Crescent Moon	128
41.	*Wasan* and *Sangaku*	131
42.	*Desmostylus*	134

43. The Ink of Kobaien   137

44. Soil and Buildings   140

45. "Oh Vreneli"   143

46. *Gekka hyōjin*   146

47. The Children's Parade   149

48. The Utility of the Adam's Apple   152

49. Graves and Meadows   155

50. A Demonstration of Dedication   158

51. Unkei and Muda Tomohiro   162

52. Hearts   165

53. A Nation's Lands   168

54. *Sontaku* and *Dangō*   171

55. Nurturing Life:
     Crows and Crouching *Dogū* Figurines   175

56. Cuckoos and Warblers   178

57. Cleaning the Pond   182

58. The Virtue of Shadows   185

59. The Attractiveness of Walls and
     Tataki Floors   188

60. Gold and Silver   192

61. *Sayōnara*   195

62. Driving in Robes   198

63. Hansōbō   202

64. A Very Local Move   206

65. Fish-Scale Paving   210

66. Scenes of the Past   213

Afterword   218

Preface to the English Edition

When asked to autograph copies of this book, I always write "Play it by ear." I believe that is the essence of living life as it comes.

The definition of "justice" in this world has always been relative to the conditions of the times. What was justice in one era commonly comes to look like corruption in another. The Japanese in particular have had to "play it by ear" over centuries of natural disasters and changing political systems. To play things by ear is to eschew rules and principles. Well, not to abandon them entirely, perhaps, but rather take a more abstract, liberal approach to their interpretation.

I believe that the Japanese have made their way by intuitively choosing the best approach to handling the "now" of each era from among a range of possibilities, including opposing dualities. Honing that intuition is one aspect of our martial arts, flower arrangement, and tea ceremony, or the trivial, repetitive acts of our everyday lives.

The problem is that when intuition weakens, this system no longer functions as intended. We simply stand confused before a multitude of options, unsure of what to do. Rather than being a sign of abundance, those options become a source of perplexity and confusion. I believe this is what dragged us toward hosting the Tokyo Olympics and Paralympics.

The archaic smile of noh masks gives them the potential to be interpreted as conveying all kinds of facial expressions, but when onstage in a particular situation, they will show only one desired expression. This is a result of the vigorous workings of the viewer's intuition in that

9

particular situation. But if you look at a noh mask with only a vague understanding of the situation the character is in, many non-Japanese find it impossible to imagine what the character is supposed to be thinking, or even feel that it looks sinister. In the meantime, the opportunity for resolution is lost.

This leads to the question of what is dulling our intuition. Part of it is certainly a decline in the practice of the above-mentioned traditions such as martial arts and tea ceremony. Perhaps the predictive powers of artificial intelligence have had some influence as well. I believe, however, that the primary cause is that while humans have recognized the preciousness of life since antiquity, if less so at some times than at others, that recognition has become particularly weak today. Simply put, what stands in opposition to life is money. Access to too much information certainly plays a role as well.

In retrospect, nearly all countries have been thinking of the number of COVID-19 cases and the health of their economies as variables to keep in balance. Perhaps that is a valid viewpoint from the perspective of society as a whole, but how can we apply that at an individual level? How can we look at human lives on the one hand and money on the other and seriously try to compare the two? Living life as it comes, with peace of mind, will require societal recognition that such a comparison is impossible. Surely countries around the world are all facing this same problem.

Just as a noh mask takes on the required expression at the required time, I hope that you will see in these writings my intuitive responses to various situations. When you see the path you are on go from zigzagging to straight, my life will have finally gained continuation within you. The question of whether human life continues after death is a major philosophical problem. Such "continuity" can also be thought of as a "story." What kind of story will emerge depends on the life you live.

I would like to thank everyone who helped with the translation of this book, and extend my gratitude to Kawaguchi Sumiko for updating her wonderful illustrations for inclusion here. I look forward to starting a relationship with my English readers.

Gen'yū Sōkyū
Summer 2021

Preface: Living Life as It Comes

These days, it often feels like things do not go the way we expect them to, causing us to become flustered. But perhaps that is because we consider it prudent to have expectations about how things should go. It has been a long time since I have seen children making *teru-teru-bōzu* charms to ward off rain, but that is probably because now we have computer simulations of what the weather will be like, and can search the Internet to see those forecasts whenever we wish.

But oh, the shock we feel when our predictions miss the mark! So much greater than if we had no expectations at all, of course. There is not much we can do about the weather. When it comes to how we behave when things do not turn out as planned, however, we often stubbornly stick with our initial expectations, insisting on "staying the course." The more effort we put into justifying our stubbornness, the harder it becomes to make changes—and the more we suffer.

Sometimes this kind of attitude is regarded as embodying a sense of responsibility, which complicates matters, but in most cases our obstinacy only brings us suffering. I often see people ending up in complete despair after repeatedly encountering unexpected circumstances, but I suppose it may be a characteristic of modern society to nonetheless continue expecting things to go a certain way.

When we stick to our guns, unswerving in our limited thinking, and things just happen to work out, we may be praised as having "resolve." However, this word in Japanese, *kokorozashi*, can also be read as "piercing the mind" or "pointing to the mind," in the sense of pinning down a mind that is too free. There are limits to the situations that can be resolved through *kokorozashi*. Natural disasters are an obvious example, but this kind of self-serving resolve also cannot do much to advance our relationships with others.

The concept of letting things work out "as they will" is sometimes viewed negatively, as irresponsible or lacking in conviction, but recognizing the processes of constant change that govern all things reflects an accurate grasp of the human condition. Little else in life is as important as this attitude, but possibly because constantly updating our worldview is too great a mental burden, we have given up and gradually come to disparage it.

It was the 2011 Tōhoku earthquake and tsunami, which had a particularly profound impact on my home prefecture of Fukushima, that made me painfully aware of the need to live life as it comes, without fixed goals, which tend to be imperfect and grounded in desire. It was not only the tsunami that was overwhelming, but also the countless unanticipated actions by those around me. After the disaster, I was asked to join the Reconstruction Headquarters and to chair a fund supporting children in my prefecture. However, I was already extremely busy supporting the many families at my temple who had experienced suicides after the disaster, and had never considered taking on new roles such as these. I was at a loss for how to respond. After a bit of moaning and groaning, however, I decided to entrust myself to the waves rather than resist them, and accepted every request made of me. Having my wife's support certainly aided this decision, but I suppose I felt like a drowning person who accepts his fate because he is powerless to avoid being dragged to the bottom.

I had realized that an undue focus on my own affairs was narrow-minded, a dam that would eventually burst. Freeing myself from the self-imposed confines of ego and sense of obligation felt like true freedom. I was in the middle of writing books including *Inori no sahō* (The Etiquette of Prayer), *Hikari no yama* (Mountain of Light), and *Mujō to iu chikara* (The Power of Evanescence), which kept me incredibly busy in a physical sense, but as soon as I gave up and let things come as they may, all the excess energy flowed out of my body, making me feel like I could take on whatever was asked of me, one request after another.

In the fall of 2007, I had appeared on an episode of the NHK television show *Shiru o tanoshimu* (Enjoy Knowing) titled "Living Life as It Comes." At the time, I was already beginning to sense the truth of that phrase, but after the 2011 disaster, I finally became certain of it.

I am reminded of a passage in the classic Taoist text *Zhuangzi*, a book I truly adore, that describes the importance of avoiding the mental stagnation of "resolve":

> If a man follows the mind given him and makes it his
> teacher, then who can be without a teacher?

In other words, we should each be following our mind as it changes according to the circumstances of the moment; it is when we devote ourselves to a fixed, already-made-up mind that things go wrong.

Zen Buddhism, too, teaches that we should neither fear the future nor regret the past, but that it takes a lot of bravery to head blindly into the future, led by an ever-changing mind. Upon reflection, however, that is all we can do. That is what life is.

The essays in this book are the product of seven or eight years of living life as it comes. Every time something happened to me during that time, I wholeheartedly embraced it as part of the ever-changing nature of the world. I discuss topics ranging from events in post-disaster Fukushima Prefecture to building temples and improving soil, along with the surprises those events brought and what they taught me. While not every essay will be directly relatable to every reader, I hope you will enjoy the journey, accompanied by the wonderful illustrations of Kawaguchi Sumiko.

As mentioned above, a life lived "as it comes" is a life of constant change. Things we accomplished two or three years ago may no longer be possible. That does not mean we must—or should—cast aside all plans for the future. The important thing is to resolve to live life as it comes, even during times of stress, accepting all so that our minds can freely operate. Even if you only manage to do this periodically, I am sure it will result in experiences that are far more valuable than the simple achievement of your plans. As the Chinese literatus Su Shì (1037–1101) wrote in a poem,

> An empty mind is infinitely rich,
> with flowers, the moon, and pavilions.

By accepting life as it comes and letting go of the self that we feel we must protect, our time in this world becomes much richer. After all, although our past was a series of unexpected events, today we recall them fondly. That is sufficient. Isn't that a good way to lead our lives?

I
We Are All the Same Age

April 2012

The essays in this book are drawn from a serial newspaper column I authored titled "*Ui no okuyama.*" This phrase is familiar to Japanese readers as part of a classic waka poem, "Iroha," which is derived from a short passage related to death in the Chinese Nirvana Sutra. We do not know who composed the Japanese poem, but whoever did is nothing short of genius, in that it retains a poetic form while also being a pangram, meaning it uses each character in the Japanese syllabary exactly once. "Iroha" is thought to have been written in the late Heian period (794–1185), and provides an excellent example of Japan's cultural maturity in that age.

The following is an English translation by Harvard professor Abe Ryūichi:

> Although its scent still lingers on
> > the form of a flower has scattered away
> For whom will the glory
> > of this world remain unchanged?
> Arriving today at the yonder side
> > of the deep mountains of evanescent existence

We shall never allow ourselves to drift away
intoxicated, in the world of shallow dreams.*

The "deep mountains of evanescent existence" is a metaphor for human life. The latter half of this poem is a description of death by one who is dying: having made the climb through a life of *ui*, the ever-changing vicissitudes of existence, the narrator has finally reached the summit and passed on to a state of *mui shizen*, or "natural stillness" (the *wu wei* of Taoism).

People of the time—or, at the very least, whoever translated this poem into Japanese—must have, like Laozi and Zhuangzi, considered the world of *mui* as superior to the world of *ui*. Having entered that world, by comparison the previous state feels like one of "intoxication" and "shallow dreams." In the state of "natural stillness," the dying person awakens to a world that can be viewed clearly, so there will be no more shallow dreams or feeling of intoxication.

During his lifetime, Siddhārtha Gautama experienced an awakening (enlightenment) through which he became a Buddha. While ordinary people like us may never experience such a transformative event, before the awakening that occurs with death, we will all experience smaller awakenings of some sort or another at least a few times.

The other day, I had the opportunity to speak with the famed physician Hinohara Shigeaki, who was one hundred years (and five months!) old when we met. I could not help but chuckle when he told me he had booked speaking engagements scheduled four to five years in the future. I quickly caught myself, however, realizing I do exactly the same thing: I make promises two years in advance, despite having no assurance I will be able to keep them. Who could say which of us will be the first to cross to the yonder side of our mountain?**

The Zen monk Sengai (1750–1837), who lived in Hakata, toward the end of his life often wrote that "we are all the same age." Death comes to both young and old. We are all the same in that sense. Last year's Tōhoku earthquake extinguished nearly twenty thousand lives, both young and old. All died at once, regardless of their age at the time.

So if you use year of death as your measure, I suppose we are indeed all the same age. But when we recall the dead, no matter how much time has passed, we remember them at the age when they died, and feel like we, too, have reverted to the age we were at the time of their death. There are fissures of natural stillness in the deep mountains of evanescent existence. Perhaps we view shallow dreams to forget that we are all the same age.

We are all the same age!!

Dr. Hinohara   Sengai

 * Abe Ryūichi, *The Weaving of Mantra: Kūkai and the Construction of Esoteric Buddhist Discourse* (New York: Columbia University Press, 2000), 398.

** Dr. Hinohara passed away five years and three months after this column appeared. It turns out he may have been able to keep all those appointments after all!

2
Soaring through Inconvenience

May 2012

I had a spell of ill health in March and April: I lost feeling in the pinky and ring finger on my left hand. I had them examined by a chiropractor, an acupuncturist, and an orthopedic doctor, but there was no improvement.

When reciting sutras in the main hall of my temple, I use my right hand to beat a wooden *mokugyo* drum and my left to strike a large gong, but I found myself unable to lift the striker. It even became difficult to tap the keys on a computer keyboard.

One of my attempted treatments left me completely unable to lift my left arm. I could not undress, could not bathe myself, and spent two nights nearly sleepless. After that, someone recommended a doctor they described as "highly skilled," so I had my deputy chief priest drive me to Date, a city in the same prefecture but still some distance away.

The doctor I met there turned out to be completely blind. After I undressed with the help of my deputy, the doctor carefully ran his fingertips over my upper body, speaking naturally in his deep voice. Having lost his sight at the age of thirteen or fourteen, his sense of touch was far more sensitive than anything I could imagine. After probing my entire back, he pointed out a problem that no one else had noticed, then took his time giving me an acupuncture treatment.

Two days after that, I happened to have the opportunity to attend a piano concert by Tsujii Nobuyuki, who is also completely blind. In 2009, Tsujii became the first Japanese winner of the Van Cliburn International Piano Competition, and has been receiving rave reviews worldwide ever since. He was on tour in support of disaster recovery, with a packed schedule that would take him through Iwate, Miyagi, Fukushima, and Akita prefectures. In response to the audience's thunderous applause, he played four encore pieces, between which he told us, "I wanted to do something to help those affected by the disaster, but I realized this is really the only skill I have." Humble words, but in them I also heard confidence. I was immediately reminded of the blind doctor I had visited, and the calm confidence he, too, had emanated.

As Tsujii sat at the piano listening to the sounds he was producing, he looked as if he were channeling Mozart or Beethoven. I suppose that the doctor, too, had used his fingers and needles to tune my body, making use of sound and feeling.

I wonder how much being blind inconveniences the two men in their daily lives. At the same time, I imagine that these two men, both masters of their craft, delved deeper into their occupations because they thought it was the only thing they could do. Through inconvenience, they learned to soar.

As you might have expected from a story like this, the day after my acupuncture treatment, the pain in my arm vanished as if it had never been there at all.

3
Flowers for the Buddha

June 2012

Empress Kōmyō (701–760) wrote the following poem:

> I pluck these flowers not for myself,
> but as an offering to the buddhas of past, present,
> and future.

Offering flowers and one's self in devotion to the Buddha is an admirable thing, but to whom were flowers first given? A lover? Okakura Kakuzō (Tenshin; 1863–1913) writes in *The Book of Tea*, "The primeval man in offering the first garland to his maiden thereby transcended the brute."* We have found remains of Neanderthals buried in graves carpeted with flowers, showing that their culture included funerary rites, if not actual religion. But regardless of who our flowers are for, humans are the only species to have developed a culture in which they are gifted.

This year once again, a parishioner of my temple passed away as the cherry blossoms bloomed in all their glory. In the past, when seeing off an elderly person who was moving on to the next world amidst a whirlwind of fluttering blossoms, I would think there is nothing else so lovely. But this man was relatively young, still in his early sixties. While

reciting a sutra by his side after he died, I could sense in his remains the pain he had suffered. Turning around, in the brightness beyond a glass door, I saw the pale pink cloud of a Yoshino cherry tree in full bloom.

As his dharma name (*kaimyō*), the name assigned to him after death, I chose Sange, which means "scattered blossoms." The word can refer both to offerings to the Buddha and to an early death. I tried to convince myself that living past fifty could be considered a full life, but I found it difficult to view the death of this man as a gentle scattering of blossoms in the breeze. He had died suddenly from a brain hemorrhage.

Certain flowers, such as camellias and trumpet vines, start to lose their petals before the flower itself has reached the end of its life. I am not sure where the custom originated, but I have seen people float those petals in a shallow water basin as a reminder to hold dear the years we have remaining to us. Focusing on such things, however, only makes us cling more tightly to what is impermanent.

I recall another passage by Okakura Kakuzō about flowers: "They are not cowards, like men. Some flowers glory in death . . ."** I imagine that when he wrote this, he was thinking of Sen no Rikyū (1522–1591), father of the Japanese tea ceremony, who had committed seppuku many years before. However, we must remember that the dead no longer suffer or worry. A scene of flowers is simply a brief flash of beauty in the mundane world.

I have heard that ikebana, the Japanese art of flower arrangement, originated among Buddhist monks. Curiously, the *ike* in ikebana means "bring to life," despite being performed on cut flowers that could have gone on happily living in the ground. Ikebana masters would toss wilted flowers into a river or bury them in the earth, saying a prayer for their spirits. Thinking of that during a funeral makes the dead seem all the more like flowers, like an offering to the Buddha.

When the deceased parishioner's son, a young man in his early thirties, spoke at the funeral I mentioned above, he said he was still unable to accept his father's death. But it is the nature of flowers to scatter to the winds, whether we want them to or not.

---

* Okakura Kakuzō, *The Book of Tea* (Carlisle: Applewood Books, 2008), 123.
** Ibid., 146.

4
The Tenacity of Five-Storied Pagodas and Prayers

July 2012

I am truly amazed at the number of five-storied pagodas Japan has produced. Among the forty-seven I was able to confirm, eleven have been designated as national treasures and fourteen registered as important cultural properties. Throw in those built purely for tourism and I am sure the number would more than double.

Pagodas evolved from stupas, which in India had a mound-like shape. When the concept of a stupa was introduced to China during the Han dynasty (206 BCE–220 CE), people began building them from wood, and before long, three- and five-storied tower-like structures appeared. The technology was transmitted to Japan via the Korean Peninsula. Today, however, there is only one left in China and one in Korea, while in Japan they have sprung up like bamboo shoots after a rain. It seems that everyone wanted their own, so they came to be constructed not just at Buddhist temples but even at Shintō shrines. I used to wonder why residents of a country as earthquake-prone as Japan would want to do such a thing.

After carefully thinking it over, however, I now wonder whether it is precisely *because* our country is so earthquake-prone that so many pagodas were built. When I tried searching for five-storied pagodas that were built but no longer exist, I could not find a single example that collapsed in an earthquake, just one that was torn down and four that burned in fires. Of the latter, the one at Tennōji Temple in Tokyo was the inspiration for Kōda Rohan's novel *The Five-Storied Pagoda*. That pagoda survived both the 1923 Great Kantō earthquake and the fire-bombing of Tokyo during World War II, yet burned in a double-suicide arson case in 1957. Such a glorious (no, inexcusable!) way for a pair of lovers to leave this world, taking a five-storied pagoda along with them!

While pagodas are vulnerable to lightning and fires, they are quite resistant to earthquakes. The oldest wooden structure in Kyoto is the five-storied pagoda at Daigoji (built in 951), which even in the Great Hanshin-Awaji earthquake of 1995 lost only a little bit of plaster from a wall. After the 2011 Tōhoku earthquake, the five-storied pagodas in nearby Aomori, Iwate, Miyagi, and Fukushima prefectures were all undamaged.

In recent years, architects have been studying the "flexible structures" of five-storied pagodas for earthquake resistance, convinced they have found a textbook for constructing earthquake-proof buildings, but

they still have a lot to learn. Even if we never discover it all, however, there is much we can learn from five-storied pagodas and their imperviousness to earthquakes.

No temple or shrine would knowingly construct a building that might collapse, crushing those inside. Five-storied pagodas therefore pose something of a challenge, daring earthquakes to just try and topple them.

The Tokyo Skytree was under construction when the Tōhoku earthquake occurred, but afterward, work on it continued without any fuss. Despite the damage to surrounding neighborhoods, it required no changes to its construction plan and seemed to be completed while our attention was elsewhere. That tower, whose design was modeled on the flexible structure of the five-storied pagoda, is another display of considerable confidence.

To me it seems that such construction projects arise from the resilience and prayers of a people who live in an earthquake-prone country, and represent the accumulation of technologies born from those prayers. In that, I feel a sense of conviction and pride.

5

Best of Health to Your Ancestors, Too

August 2012

I have been involved in a series of reburial ceremonies of late. Specifically, remains interred in my temple's graveyard are being transferred to other locations. Removing cremated remains that are housed in an above-ground crypt is simple, but in some cases the urns are buried underground, and occasionally the deceased were buried without being cremated. The stoneworker who digs them up has a tough job.

A stoneworker who appeared to be in his mid-seventies came for the reburial we held today. After digging all morning, he came to me, drenched in sweat, saying "I've only found one urn. How many more were you expecting?"

"I'm not really sure," I said, shaking my head and recalling the row of gravestones that had been there. "We're supposed to be moving the lot of them. You haven't found any more?"

"I haven't," he said. "I've dug pretty deep and stuck a probe into the dirt, but I'm not hitting anything."

Lack of cremation urns likely meant burial directly in the earth. That would mean digging to a depth of a couple of meters, despite there being a strong possibility that no bones remained.

Looking at the exhausted stoneworker, I said, "I suppose all we'd find is dirt."

"I imagine so," he replied.

He then brought another urn, approximately the same size as the one he had uncovered, and filled it with dirt from the grave.

That afternoon I was visited by the daughter of the last person buried in that grave, already eighty years old herself. She was accompanied by her own daughter, who appeared to be in her forties. The former had married into another family but continued to maintain the graves of the family she had been born into. Her husband had been buried at his family's gravesite, however, and taking care of both was no doubt difficult. This reburial was actually a joining of the ancestors of two families into a single gravesite while the grave owner was still healthy enough to do so.

After I finished reciting the requisite sutra, the woman's first words were "Oh my, I don't think we can carry all that." It turned out her daughter was going to be carrying the remains back home on the Shinkansen bullet train, so she could only manage one of the large

urns. After some thinking, we ended up transferring a portion of the soil to a small urn normally used when cremated remains are split among multiple parties. This made the remains portable enough for her to manage.

But isn't it interesting, I thought, how attached we Japanese can be to our ancestors' remains? And yet those "remains" we are so obsessed with may be nothing more than an urn filled with dirt! We may even be unsure of the details, such as how many ancestors are supposedly contained within that dirt!

Before they left, bearing their urns of remains and soil, the woman and her daughter bowed deeply before the temple's Buddha and said, "Thank you for watching over our ancestors for such a long time." As I watched them leave, I could not help but feel like the proprietor of a boarding house, happily cheering for a long-time resident who was moving on after finding a job.

Remember that we do not pass our time here only among the living. Wish for the best of health to your ancestors, too.

6

Human Rights

September 2012

I would like to consider some new developments connected with human rights. Recently the concept of "smoke-haters' rights" for people who dislike cigarettes has gone mainstream. "Smokers' rights" have long been on thin ice, but this seems like an area in which neither side can find room for mutual respect and coexistence. Maybe recognizing a "right to hate" has affirmed individual judgments regarding superiority and inferiority, right and wrong, thereby making haters feel as if they have been awarded the right to make such judgments.

Recently, I have also seen online talk of "dog haters' rights." This will likely come as a surprise to those who have pet dogs, but there are people in the world who not only dislike dogs but also hate their owners. Read into that a little more deeply and you come to see rights for hating dogs as well as those who love them.

So far, there has been no legal recognition of dog haters' rights. This is likely because keeping cats, dogs, and other pets is not yet seen as "interfering with the public welfare," but who can say what the future will bring? There was a time when cigarettes were considered as medicine for preventing colds.

Regardless of whether you are speaking of dogs or cigarettes, loving them and hating them may seem like two sides of the same coin, but actually they are quite different attitudes: while in most cases the lovers do not hate the haters, the haters generally hate the lovers. Furthermore, this hatred entails no effort by the hater.

Article 13 of Japan's constitution has a lot to say about human rights: "All of the people shall be respected as individuals. Their right to life, liberty, and the pursuit of happiness shall, to the extent that it does not interfere with the public welfare, be the supreme consideration in legislation and in other governmental affairs."* All good so far, but some big questions remain, such as how to distinguish between "pursuit of happiness" and mere desire, and how to determine standards for judging "the public welfare."

Since the nuclear accident caused by the tsunami following the Tōhoku earthquake, many residents of Fukushima Prefecture have been trying to gain recognition for their right to hate radiation. It sure seems that if we can recognize one's right to hate smoke, there should be rights for hating radiation, or noise from military bases.

I suppose such rights are not awarded because "the right to hate" never solves anything. Our inability to decide what to do about interim

storage facilities for radiation-contaminated materials, the recent pro-
tests against debris processing . . . these are all related to "the right to
hate."

But we must not forget that rights and responsibilities come as a pair.
There is plenty of potential for "the right to hate" to itself "interfere with
the public welfare." It could also become a free pass to whip out when
one is upset about something. There is no question that human rights
have become a complex issue in today's world.

---

* https://japan.kantei.go.jp/constitution_and_government_of_japan/
constitution_e.html

7
Taboo Words

November 2012

In Japan, students approaching school entrance exams avoid using words like "fail" and "flunk" as best they can. Not only do they avoid using those words, they try to not even hear or see them. If you were a Japanese student with an important test coming up, you might have already quit reading by now.

The Japanese word for "reed" is *ashi*, but that is a homophone with another word meaning "evil," so some people instead confusingly call the plant *yoshi*, which means "good." I am sure there are many people in Japan who are unaware that *yoshi* and *ashi* are the same plant. Another example of this is calling dried squid both *surume* and *atarime*, replacing *suru* ("to lose," as in when gambling) with *ataru* ("to win"), and similarly calling grinding mortars both *suribachi* and *ataribachi*. These examples show the Japanese belief in the power of words, which we also have a word for: *kotodama*, or "language spirits."

Some taboo words are peculiar to specific eras. During World War II, all words derived from English were associated with the enemy, making the entire language taboo. This put the very survival of baseball (which originated in the US) in doubt, so supporters quickly found native replacements for English words like "strike," "out," and "player,"

suribachi surume ashi
ataribachi atarime yoshi

particularly words that emphasized a patriotic "fighting spirit." Considering the popularity of baseball and other aspects of American culture in Japan today, it feels as if that was a completely different world.

During the Kamakura period (1185–1333), certain taboo words were specific to a particular imperial residence. Some of these are quite interesting, so I would like to introduce a few of them.

The Saigū was a member of the imperial family, usually an unmarried princess, who served at Ise Shrine on behalf of an acceding emperor. She would perform ablutions in the river there, and spend a year cloistered in a building called Nonomiya, performing purification ceremonies. During that time, she and her attendants would be required to strictly adhere to restrictions on the words they could use.

As one serving the gods and praying for a safe accession, she would of course avoid "unclean" language, but many Buddhist terms were also replaced with other words. For example, she would say "fix" in place of "die," "rest" instead of "illness," "tiled roof" instead of "temple," "yew" instead of "tower," "clods of earth" instead of "grave," and "dyed paper" rather than "sutra."

An impressive effort, I must say, but some of the substitutions were even more curious. In particular, I understand that these vestal virgin princesses referred to monks as "long-hairs" and the Buddha as the "child within." Referring to shaven-headed monks as "long-hairs" is downright silly, but I find the "child within" term especially intriguing. One explanation is that [a statue of] the Buddha was always kept enclosed within a miniature shrine, making him "the child within." Yoshida Kenkō (1283–1350) commented on this in *Tsurezuregusa* (Essays in Idleness), not criticizing the practice but finding it endearing: "The seclusion of the high priestess at Nonomiya was a most refined and delightful thing. It is also interesting that she must avoid Buddhist words such as 'sutra' or 'the Buddha,' replacing them with 'dyed paper' and 'child within.'" He goes on to describe the scenery of the shrines themselves and how attractive he found them. Yoshida praises such cultural ingenuity, in which those embodying the taboo cloister themselves, describing it as a "refined and delightful thing," surpassing divinity itself.

If replacing a taboo word with a substitute indicates recognition and acceptance of the existence of that word's power, does that mean "nuclear power" (*genpatsu*) has not yet been accepted as a taboo word? While I have heard people mistakenly use the word "nuclear bomb" (*genbaku*) in its place, I have yet to hear anyone use an alternative term.

8

Colds and Their Benefits

December 2012

In his book *Colds and Their Benefits*, Noguchi Haruchika (1911–1976) argued that catching a cold now and then is a good thing. The author survived the Great Kantō earthquake when he was twelve years old, during which he says he healed a person simply by holding his hands over the injured area. The experience inspired him to become a healer, and eventually he went on to develop a unique method of healing called Noguchi Seitai. What I want to discuss here, however, is nothing quite so grandiose, just that every time I catch a cold I am reminded of *Colds and Their Benefits*.

I suppose one could take the gutsy position that if you are going to catch a cold, you might as well find some benefit in the experience, but I suspect that in fact, we catch colds because something within us decides that catching one would be a fine thing to do, and we therefore let down our guard. I recently recovered from my first cold in several years, and as to why I let my guard down, I blame a dreamlike time I spent in Kanazawa.

In October, I visited Kanazawa to attend an event commemorating the first anniversary of the opening of a museum dedicated to the Buddhist teacher and philosopher D.T. Suzuki (1870–1966). I happened to be giving a lecture in Kyoto before that, leaving me a whole day before I needed to be in Kanazawa, so having heard about a good hot spring inn there, I arrived a day early.

Indeed, the Motoyu Ishiya inn at Fukatani Hot Springs was a wonderfully relaxing place. To start with, the hot spring itself, first discovered by the Buddhist monk Gyōki (668–749), is amazing. The hot water that comes bubbling up from underground through accumulated organic matter is not the amber color one normally sees, but nearly black due to oxidation. I had heard of a similar hot spring in Hokkaido but had never gone to one myself. Experiencing something for the first time always intrigues me; I lost count of how many times I bathed that day.

The meals were also wonderful. The dishes were exquisite, and there was a wide variety of saké. My server was a delight too, a young man who had recently joined the staff. Best of all, however, was the ninety-six-year-old proprietor, a so-called *myōkōnin*. You can read more about *myōkōnin* in D.T. Suzuki's writings, but briefly stated, they are pious laypersons in the Jōdo Shinshū sect of Buddhism. He explained the history of the place and its treasures, gave me a tour of the two noh stages there, and even related stories of his school principal when he was a child, leaving me profoundly impressed. Then he suddenly leapt up, scurried off, and returned with towels for me and my wife, saying, "Please enjoy the bath."

Imagine my stunned expression the next morning when he came up to us and apologized, saying "I'm sorry I wasn't myself yesterday, I had a slight fever." Have you ever met a ninety-six-year-old who can scamper up and down hotel hallways with a 38.6°C (101.5°F) fever?

Lulled by the hot springs and the food and the saké, I totally let my guard down and did not truly see the elderly man I had been speaking with. Therefore this is not just a trifling story about me catching his cold. (Though I am sure part of me had wanted to from the beginning.)

I made it through the talk and symposium at the D.T. Suzuki Museum without any real symptoms, but I spent the day after returning to my temple in bed. I remain unsure as to what benefit I got from that cold, but despite being all better now, I cannot shake the image of that old man dashing about.

9

The Chrysanthemum and the Sword and Duality

January 2013

I cannot help but feel that the Japanese have long had a strange predilection for maintaining dualities of opposing extremes. One example is how we use both Chinese characters (kanji) and our own native syllabaries (kana) to write our language. Not only that, but apparently being unsatisfied with just one syllabary, we use two. The kana are strictly phonetic, allowing for immediate conversion of symbols into sounds, while our brains recognize the kanji as something more like pictures. From what I understand, there are few languages in the world that use both systems.

While Japanese culture exalts a compact, austere lifestyle exemplified by hermitages (*iori*) and Zen temple abbot's quarters (*hōjō*), our architecture also includes heroic castles. We love transience and imperfection embodied in *wabi/sabi*, but our society also produced mentalities such as *date* (flamboyance) and *basara* (pretentiousness). We Japanese have thus lived with an eye toward pairs of extremes—Japanese style and Chinese style, duty and sentiment—without much concern for unifying them.

Castle-dwellers are a different sort from monastery-dwellers. An individual cannot practice both *basara* and *wabi*. While the whole includes both polarities, there are certainly cases where the individual must choose one or the other. Then again, there are also many cases like duty and sentiment, or true feelings (*honne*) and publicly expressed feelings (*tatemae*), where both exist within an individual in a state of ongoing contention. Indeed, it is impossible to live one's life by duty or sentiment alone, and most Japanese consider both *honne* and *tatemae* to be necessary.

The American anthropologist-folklorist Ruth Benedict (1887–1948) pointed out such contradictions in Japanese society in her book *The Chrysanthemum and the Sword*. How is it, she asked, that the kind-hearted people who treasure the delicate chrysanthemum can also have such respect for the sword that would cut it in half? Benedict jokingly states that contradiction is part of the warp and weft of the Japanese people, but why pay particular attention to writings by an author who never actually visited Japan? She probably had only a superficial understanding of this country where contradictions are a source of energy.

Another duality

Not that I bear a grudge against Dr. Benedict, but I think her not being familiar with the concept of duality that derives from the Chinese *Zhuangzi* is the downfall of her theories. It was Japan's embrace of duality that allowed it to comfortably grasp the "middle way" of Buddhism. Furthermore, our recognition of opposing extremes is what allows for tolerance.

Some claim Benedict wrote *The Chrysanthemum and the Sword* at the behest of the US government to justify dropping atomic bombs on Japan. Whether or not that is the case, I believe we can feel a bit more confident in our culture by recognizing not its "contradictions" but its duality. Then again, since we are a culture of duality, we are also free to not have confidence.

10
The Boat on the Hill

February 2013

I recently visited some disaster sites for the first time in a while—Kesennuma, Onagawa, Ishinomaki, and others. At each site, the mounds of rubble formed from what had once been objects used by residents in their daily lives were now cleared away, leaving stark, empty fields.

One particularly remarkable scene from my tour was an enormous boat, several tens of meters in length, that had wound up in the middle of a former residential area in Kesennuma. Although the boat was registered in Iwaki, Fukushima Prefecture, the tsunami had dragged it an unbelievable distance inland and left it there, nearly upright. When I saw it, the boat even had supports keeping it in that position. Although countless boats ran aground throughout the disaster area, this was the only one that had not yet been removed, I was told.

Some locals suggested that the boat should remain where it was as a reminder of the awesome power of tsunamis. Others wanted it removed, calling it a hindrance to reconstruction, a source of fear, and a reminder of lost relatives. I spoke about this with Onodera Yūji, director of the Kesennuma Reconstruction Village, who said, "I can see how it might bring back bad memories for some, but the boat is a victim, too." Apparently, he was in favor of leaving it where it was.

The Reichstag building in Germany has great architectural value, but anyone who sees it cannot help but recall films of Hitler giving speeches from its balcony. Perhaps that is why the artists Christo and Jeanne-Claude wrapped the entire structure as an art installation. Wrapping the building transformed it into something else, they said, providing an emotional detachment that allowed people to view it with fresh eyes. Onodera's comments came after I told him of this.

It is an interesting perspective. While Hitler and the 2011 tsunami were both highly destructive forces, the Reichstag and the stranded ship played different roles in those events, and thus occupy different positions today. The Reichstag was a source of Hitler's power, while the boat was simply a fishing vessel that had been cast ashore. Viewers of the ship may feel a fear of tsunamis, but they would not feel a hatred of boats.

There is a similar ship in Indonesia that was left in place and even transformed into a tsunami museum. Could that happen here? Could the Japanese people, or at least the people of the Tōhoku region, con-

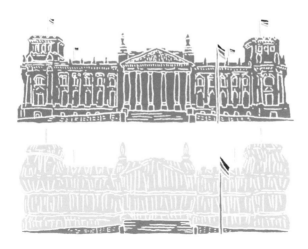

sider such resilience itself to be acting with grace? I am not sure of the answer, and since attitudes toward disaster recovery vary so widely, I suspect there is no simple solution.

The land near the seaside has been reduced to open fields, and no building will be possible there without raising the ground. That had not yet started on a regional scale at the time of my visit, due to land ownership issues. Instead, those unable to wait for regional construction were braving the snow in dump trucks to haul in soil to raise their own land.

The "boat on the hill" seems to be a symbol of the frustration that many people in this region are feeling. In the classical thirteenth-century essay collection *Hōjōki*, Kamo no Chōmei writes that those who are quick to rebuild things as something new are also quick to forget the dead. Perhaps frustration is the true badge of integrity among disaster victims.*

---

* Disassembly of the boat described above started on 9 September 2013, and it has since been removed.

11
Efficiency and Harmony

March 2013

The other day, my wife and I visited Amami Ōshima, one of the islands between Okinawa and Kyushu. I of course enjoyed the warm weather, as well as the different approach to work I saw there.

A woman from the hotel where we were staying came to meet us at the airport, and when we arrived at the hotel, a congenial man who appeared to be in his forties came out to greet us. Both wore relatively casual attire instead of the suits common in the Japanese hospitality business.

While we were sitting in chairs, waiting in the lobby, the man brought us tea. He kindly showed us around the building and told us about nearby sightseeing spots and the weather at that time of year. For dinner, they served a traditional chicken and rice dish, after which I had to do some work, correcting a manuscript that a publisher had faxed to the hotel. When I was done, I took it to the front desk to ask them to fax it back for me.

Up to this point, everything was similar to what I would expect back on the mainland. At the front desk, though, I was surprised to see the hotel chef, whom I had just spoken with in the dining room. In fact, he was the only one working the desk! As I stood there, uncertain as to whether it was appropriate to ask the hotel chef if I could use the fax machine, he turned to me and said, "Need the fax, do you? Sure, no problem." I handed the manuscript to him and told him where to send it, but something about the whole exchange felt very strange.

I was even more surprised the next morning. My wife said she wanted to see the hotel's collection of Ōshima-tsumugi, a silk textile the island is famous for, so we visited the display room there. Our guide turned out to be the woman who had picked us up at the airport the previous day. When my wife asked a question she could not answer, the woman said, "I'll bring someone who knows more about it," and she soon returned with the man who had served us tea. He turned out to know quite a lot about the subject, and upon asking why, I learned that he had once been a dealer in Ōshima-tsumugi fabrics, and that he was now the hotel's manager. When I ordered a massage after dinner, the woman who had picked us up was also my masseuse.

The next day, we visited the Ōshima-tsumugi Museum, where we

learned that while several weavers are usually on-site giving demonstrations, it was currently the busy season at the local sugarcane plant, so they were there helping out. I started wondering if anybody on this island held just one job.

Thinking more about it, I realized the people here were practicing the ancient Japanese workstyle. While I am sure efficiency improves when people who are proficient at the same task are grouped together, the resulting increase in competitiveness dilutes social harmony. By contrast, when everyone is swapping jobs, they understand the suffering that each task entails, so harmony is maintained.

In the end it is a question of division of labor, something I hear the Japanese post office is struggling with even today. Workplace harmony seems to be inversely proportional to the degree of division of labor in a given workplace. I would never expect a hotel manager to serve me tea on the mainland, but I am happy in the knowledge that such people exist.

12

Campbell-sensei

May 2013

There are some people in this world who are truly amazing. One is Dr. Robert Campbell, a professor of Japanese literature at Waseda University who makes frequent media appearances in Japan. I once had the pleasure of having him visit my temple for a television shoot.

Standing there in the entranceway, he easily read the calligraphic writing on a *tsuitate* single-panel screen, a feat few Japanese would be capable of. This was not the result of some challenge I posed to him. The screen was just standing there, so I suppose he naturally considered it a target of interest. Now this, I thought, is a man of culture.

The character he read was 関 (*kan*), which can mean both "barrier" and "gateway," and in Zen Buddhism refers to the start of Zen studies. It was a masterful example of calligraphy by Furukawa Taikō, an abbot of the Myōshinji school of Rinzai Zen. I had been surprised to learn he created it when he was ninety-eight years old, just two months before his death. I was even more surprised when Dr. Campbell effortlessly read it.

Still in shock, I guided Dr. Campbell to the temple study, where he stopped again to read the scrolls hanging there. After staring for a while at a calligraphy reading "The deep snow portends one hundred blessings," he peered at the artist's seal and, again reading it effortlessly, asked "Who is Mumon?" He was asking about Yamada Mumon (1900–1988), another Myōshinji abbot. After I explained this, he nodded and asked, "By one hundred blessings, I suppose he means *fuki* [butterbur] flower buds?"

Actually when thinking about what blessings might be hidden within deep snow, I had imagined plum blossoms, the simplest answer. But come to think of it, *fuki* buds—one of the most beloved edible wild plants in Japan, often melting holes in the snow as they emerge in great numbers in early spring—would be an equally good answer.

It felt as if a gust of spring wind was blowing from Dr. Campbell, as if I had been freed from fetters that had restrained me for many years.

We spoke for far longer than what was shown on television. While I am not one to use the sensei honorific lightly, it felt completely natural to call him "Campbell-sensei," or just "sensei." Nothing else seemed right! He also surprised me with his deep understanding of my book *Hikari no yama* (Mountain of Light), which he had kindly read before we met. I ordered some of his books as soon as he left.

That evening I received a thank-you email from Dr. Campbell, written in perfect Japanese, in which he also sent me a link to an animated version of the *rakugo* story *Atama-yama* (Mt. Head) that he recommended. Between the thrill of having met Dr. Campbell and the excitement of watching *Atama-yama*, I did not get much sleep that night. At least, that is what I wish I could say. Truth is, I slept like a baby.

13

A Country in Need of Constant Tending

June 2013

This is the season in which I feel the robust vitality of nature. Sprouting plants in early spring have a joyous feel, and for a time we had enjoyed the varied shades of new greenery, but by this point all of that has mellowed. Now, unwanted branches are sprouting from where the trees were pruned and must be cut back. In the fields and rice paddies and at the temple, the weeds and grasses are growing aggressively. I have given up on pulling weeds on the temple grounds, and now just mow them, making them think they have been snapped by a strong wind. Doing so suppresses their growth while improving their cooling effect.

This reminds me of hair, another thing that requires constant tending. I shave my head daily, but the hair just keeps growing back, despite my cutting it off far more frequently and aggressively than I weed the gardens or prune the trees.

Long ago when my grandfather, also abbot of our temple, was getting older, he tired of always having to shave his head, so he painted his scalp with egg whites, then vigorously dried it with a towel. The heat from the friction would bake his hair follicles, someone had told him, preventing the hair from growing back. I am not sure how much of an effect that treatment had, but I seem to recall him eventually abandoning that method and letting my grandmother shave his pate clean. I think my grandfather had given up, realizing that when you are dealing with nature, you have to maintain a basic attitude of "tending." There is simply no way around it.

In ancient Japan, the characters for "hair," "tree," and "spirit" were all pronounced *ke*, in praise of the power of self-renewal found in each. Those long-ago people thought that pulling a hair created a god, and that gods resided in trees. This was part of the Shintō understanding of nature's reproductive power. The worst thing, to them, was atrophy of that reproductive power (*ke*), which they associated with spiritual corruption. They considered it best to live alongside natural things while tending them somewhat so as to prevent their reproductive power from drying up and allowing them to become corrupt. Perhaps it is this love and respect for reproductive power that shaped the Japanese attitude toward nature.

Recently I have seen people pruning the branches of ginkgo trees before they drop their leaves, because sweeping up after them is such a nuisance. I have even heard of people laying concrete to prevent weeds from growing. I hear about things like that all the time. But when you

go to such extremes, it seems as if you are giving up all the benefits just to avoid a little inconvenience.

This is now becoming an issue in the construction of seawalls along Japan's coast. Namely, the government is building seawalls so high that while we are spared some of the burden the sea imposes on us, we are also blocking out much of its bounty.

A head with follicles baked so that its hairs stop growing is no longer a monk's head. Similarly, a Japan surrounded by high seawalls is no longer the country it once was. Unlike my grandfather's eccentric experiment, that is something I cannot laugh about.

14
Snake Eyes

August 2013

I have had many opportunities to visit Gifu Prefecture of late—three times just in the last month or so. I held services and gave talks at Daikōji Temple, gave a summer course lecture at Shōgenji, and in between had a public dialogue with the mayor of the city of Gifu and Koide Nobuaki, president of the *Chūnichi Shimbun* newspaper. During two of those three visits, local products from my hometown of Miharu were exhibited, for which I am very grateful.

The Gifu area is famous for cormorant fishing, paper lanterns, and *janome* (snake-eye) umbrellas. While there, I saw many large billboards advertising those umbrellas. At first the design reminded me of an *ensō*—a circle often used in connection with Zen Buddhism. People assign various meanings to *ensō*, but the most important is that there is no moment of stillness in a circle. While the circle itself is a restraint, its form allows no hint of inertia; it is a continuation of active, free creation that just happens to take a circular shape. Gifu Prefecture is home to so many Rinzai-school Buddhist temples that it has been called "Rinzai Kingdom," so perhaps one day a priest in the area drew a circle on his umbrella that became what is now known as *janome*.

But why refer to it as a "snake-eye"? Long ago, snakes were considered incarnations of earth spirits. Hunters in particular worshipped snakes as high-ranking gods. This is nothing but supposition, but perhaps when farming societies and hunting societies collide, respecting each other's gods is the first step toward achieving harmony. So maybe the snake-eye design is a stern reminder not to forget our previous lifestyle as hunters.

I understand that there was no such thing as murder when our ancestors were living a hunter-gatherer lifestyle. Such malice, it seems, arose only after we invented granaries that could store our harvests, giving rise to the concept of property. Much has changed since then, to the point where we consider even the land and sea as things that can be owned, and crime has only gotten worse.

When I was a child, I daydreamed about how in the future people would not need to carry things like umbrellas around with them. In this imagined age of Astro Boy, all they would have to do is press a button to instantly get whatever they wanted. The wisdom of humankind has not realized that future, however. Umbrellas still exist as they have for so long, mixing form and function in their designs.

I grew up hearing the phrase "peace under the nuclear umbrella," but today that, too, feels as empty as a childhood dream. A society that knows the horror of Hiroshima and Nagasaki can view the use of nuclear weapons only as an act of evil. If we could assure ourselves that such a dangerous umbrella would never be used, we would have no need for it. But I imagine the cool eyes of a snake gazing upon the stupidity of humanity, which finds it hard to resist using the weapons it has obtained.

15

Equinoxes and Obon

September 2013

Having finally made it through Obon, a busy time for Buddhist priests in Japan, I find myself on the brink of the autumnal equinox. I suppose I am biased, but both certainly seem to have become national events. For many people, however, they are just occasions for visiting the family gravesite, so I would like to spend a little time considering their more fundamental meaning.

Equinoxes are those days when day and night have equal duration, with the sun rising directly to the east and setting directly to the west. This makes them the perfect opportunity for contemplating the "Pure Land" (paradise) of Pure Land Buddhism, a realm said to lie beyond the setting sun. As you can experience by attempting it yourself, creating a particularly powerful image in your mind through meditative contemplation leads you to a world in which values and judgments are completely dissociated. Discrimination between good and evil, beauty and ugliness, superiority and inferiority, and the like—a task we can normally perform without effort—loses its potency when we pursue a visualized image.

Buddhism describes that state as "nondiscrimination" (*mufunbetsu*) and teaches us that from it arises the type of spiritual knowledge called "nondiscriminatory wisdom" (Jp. *mufunbetsu-chi*; Sk. *nirvikalpa-jñāna*). The world when viewed from this perspective is the "Pure Land." By contrast, Obon is on its surface a time when spirits of the dead are said to return to this world, but when they do so, it is not the everyday world that they visit. In something akin to "opening the gates of Hell," the countless lives that we have ignored or destroyed for the sake of our own convenience are released for the duration of Obon.

It goes without saying that convenience is normally our priority in everyday life. While we pay lip service to the ideal that all lives are precious, and thus that we should not kill, it is impossible to extend that compassion equally to pests and vermin, flies and mosquitos, viruses, and bacteria.

Indeed, Obon originated in China as a ceremony recognizing the human tendency to show favoritism toward our own children despite knowing it would be better to love all equally. The story goes that the mother of Maudgalyayana, one of the closest disciples of the Buddha, thought of herself as having only a limited amount of love, so that any love she felt for others would reduce the amount she could devote to her child. For this sin of miserliness, she was reborn as a "hungry ghost"

(Jp. *gaki*; Sk. *preta*) in one of the Six Realms of Existence. From this began the Japanese ritual of *segaki*, or "feeding the hungry ghosts," in which the living offer food for any wandering hungry ghosts during Obon. Still, humans are likely incapable of avoiding favoritism.

Today, there is little room for the dead in our daily lives; it is just too difficult to conveniently work them in. That is why we celebrate Obon, a limited period of "charity" toward the countless entities we usually can find no time for, the dead included. Like the equinox, it is a time for equality during which we do not discriminate between the living and the dead, between our children and the children of others. Both Obon and the equinox are special times for setting our own convenience aside, and for giving our discrimination a break.

16
Decaying Homes

October 2013

In early September I visited Tomioka, a town here in Fukushima Prefecture that was contaminated by radioactive fallout during the nuclear power plant accident that resulted from the Tōhoku earthquake and tsunami. The area is now classified as a restricted residence zone. Supposedly I was taking ten members and alumni of a theological research committee of the Myōshinji school temples in Kyoto—the head temple of the school to which my temple belongs—on a tour through the disaster area. However, because I know very little about Tomioka, our real guide was a man who was currently living in temporary housing in Miharu but whose home was in the restricted residence zone. He was eighty-four years old but still quite spry.

It took about an hour and a half by minibus from the Miyakoji district of Tamura to our guide's now uninhabited home, which is close to the Tomioka town office. We arrived at dusk, but I could see that the grass in his garden was neatly trimmed and the trees well pruned. When I mentioned this, he said his son and daughter-in-law had come by a week before to tidy things up for us. I felt guilty for burdening them with our visit.

While our guide was going back to get his house key, which he had

forgotten on the bus, the committee members pulled out the dosimeters we had issued them and started taking measurements near the ground. "I've got three microsieverts here!" one said. "Four over here!" said another. When we had passed through Kawauchi around half an hour earlier, the readings had been around 0.2 microsieverts, so their surprise was understandable.

As soon as we entered our guide's house, I lit incense at his home altar and recited a sutra for his parents and grandparents, whose photographs were displayed there. There were no leaks in the roof, and someone was coming back to the house every forty days or so, so the place was not in bad shape. Even so, while reciting the sutra I felt sorry that everyone in that region had been deprived of a place where their ancestors could rest in peace.

I saw many cars and bicycles left in front of abandoned homes throughout the residential area. All the houses were surrounded by tall grass, and the nearby "difficult-to-return" zone (a stricter level of restriction) looked like it was sinking into a sea of weeds.

I saw new homes and old homes, large estates and small apartments, even convenience stores. All looked like lifeless cells in tissue drained of its lifeblood. Alongside the tracks of the Jōban train line were huge swellings of overgrown weeds and shrubs, completely hiding the tracks like some enormous serpent. The entire town was covered in an unbroken expanse of wild vegetation.

While our guide seemed in good health, he said he sometimes felt a weakness in his abdomen. To me, that sounded like a lessened will to live, like every time something reminded him of these decaying homes, or when he imagined them, it just sapped all his energy.

People have a surprising ability to utilize even the small things as a reason for living. If the powers that be are capable of imagining the suffering of those who have had even that stripped from them, I hope they will officially decide not to restart our nuclear power plants, at the very least those in Fukushima, and certainly not for something so frivolous as producing power for the 2020 Tokyo Olympics.

17
The Price of Economizing

November 2013

Allow me to tell you about something that happened to a friend of mine. He was invited to a recital of *shigin* chanting of poetry—an art form he had never seen before, despite being in his fifties—so he and the person who invited him took a sightseeing bus to Tokyo.

He said everything had gone smoothly until they made it to Tokyo, when the bus suddenly stopped in front of a bridge near the event venue. As he watched, the bus conductor hurried off the vehicle without any explanation for why they had stopped. The conductor did not return for some time, during which a line of cars formed behind them, honking their horns. The passengers remained on the bus in a state of near panic, not knowing what was going on.

Eventually, they learned that the bus had a height of 3.7 meters, and the bridge where they stopped had only 3.5 meters clearance. So they had a bridge that was a full twenty centimeters too low in front of them, and a string of cars behind them, making both progress and retreat impossible. If you were the driver or the conductor, what would you have done?

As you might imagine, someone eventually called the police. Three officers showed up in a patrol car and a fourth came by bicycle. They blocked off the street and guided the cars backward one at a time until there was room for the bus to back out of its predicament.

The bus driver was not fined or charged with anything, but there had been a large sign 300 meters before the bridge, warning of the low clearance ahead. It therefore would not have been much of a stretch to pin the blame on the bus company staff for not having sufficiently vetted the route.

Furthermore, after having escaped from that tight spot, once they got very close to the venue, the bus driver entered a road so narrow it made the passengers nervous. My friend suspects the driver was using a navigation system meant for passenger vehicles, but whatever the cause, they soon found themselves unable to proceed, due to a car that had parked on the street. This being Tokyo, of course they already had a line of cars behind them. While the driver had managed to garner some sympathy during the bridge incident, by this point the passengers had pretty much had enough. They decided to just get off where they were and briskly walk the rest of the way.

My friend, who had arranged the transportation, told me he had gotten quotes from three bus companies and picked one that seemed in-

credibly cheap. From this, he said, he learned an important lesson about the dangers of simply going with the lowest bidder.

Nowadays, everything seems to be a competition for cheapness. But once you have reached a certain point, you cannot make things cheaper without sacrificing something important: your employees' sleep, the salary you pay them, and if that is not enough, then the experience you would normally demand when hiring. I am glad my friend made it back in one piece, because safety is invaluable. You don't need to pay more than necessary, but don't put your life on the line for a too-low price!

18

The Feeling of Freshness

January 2014

For many years, my temple has not had a bell to ring at midnight when the New Year arrives, as many temples do, so our tradition has been to instead hold a Zen meditation session early on New Year's morning. I have been leading it for over thirty years now.

Traditional Buddhist practice on the morning of January 1 is to make offerings of pure water to the deities enshrined in the main and Kannon halls, and to recite the Perfection of Wisdom (*Daihannya*) sutra. We do these things whether there are visitors to the temple or not, so we figured we might as well make an event of it.

It is hard to predict what the weather will be like on January 1. Once, I had to shovel snow at midnight, two, and four in the morning, and once, our parking lot froze over. I always hope there will not be strong winds, but things do not always go as we wish. Regardless of the weather, I start meditating at around five o'clock to calm myself, then open up the doors to the main hall at around five thirty. I also go around turning off the space heaters, which will have been running since around four o'clock.

We call this practice "reinvigorating the spirit," and while meditating in that environment is a somewhat masochistic experience, our regulars

say there is something addictive about it. It is not all that bad if the wind is not blowing, but when the wind is strong, it can be pretty rough. Either way, no trace of warmth remains in the drafty hall; that is replaced in an instant by perfect silence and frigid air.

When your mind reaches a state of total nonresponsiveness and you can sit with a stillness like a frozen tree in winter, you start to feel a warmth ignite somewhere deep within your body, as if experiencing heat for the first time. The warmth seems to have come in from the outside, carried on the freezing wind, yet it also feels as if a new flame of life has been ignited within a body whose flame was once snuffed out by those winds. A painful illusion, perhaps, but one that feels like starting over from the beginning, a creation of light within utter darkness.

The New Year is a time for mending, a chance to iron out the irregularities that arose over the previous year. That is why all Zen temples display scrolls bearing images of Bodhidharma (Jp. Daruma), the founder and first patriarch of Zen Buddhism, at this time of year. Normally I do not make New Year's resolutions or use the holiday to otherwise set goals for the year. I simply consider it a chance to reset myself, allowing me to make judgments in a natural state according to the circumstances of the time. As a resident of Fukushima Prefecture, however, it is hard these days to ignore political goings-on. Even I find myself wanting to set goals. With the embers of the earthquake still smoldering, I wish we could go around turning off the heaters (the nuclear power plants) for good this time, and sit in the cold for a while to think about where we head from here.

The doors are flung open, but our heaters remain lit. Cold and warm air are mixing together, leaving things lukewarm. What we need is the feeling of freshness that can arise only from ultimate stillness and harsh cold. Bodhidharma is watching us with that fierce glare of his, asking, "What could possibly be more important?"

19

Solicitations

February 2014

At the beginning of the New Year, I had to create a *kanjinchō*. When most Japanese hear this word, they think of a famous kabuki play of the same name, but what I am talking about here is an actual document: a solicitation of donations for the construction and repair of a temple or shrine.

In the play, there is a scene where the protagonist Benkei needs to convince someone he is a Buddhist priest, so he pretends to read from a blank scroll as if it is an actual *kanjinchō*. I wish I could do so with the aplomb of Benkei, but for me it is quite a task to write an appeal for the Enichisan Fukujūji Temple, including episodes from its near seven-hundred-year history, praise for those who have protected and repaired it over that time, and a description of how it is now falling into disrepair.

Actually, we had started preparations for a fundraising drive in the year of the Tōhoku earthquake, but since most of our parishioners were disaster victims themselves, 2011 turned out to be a bad time to ask them for donations. Despite my living quarters at the temple being officially deemed "partially destroyed," with some doors no longer able to be opened, three years passed before we felt comfortable making any such request.

I was afraid some parishioners might complain that even three years after the disaster was too soon, but we just could not wait any longer to do something about the roof. When we last painted the buildings, we were told the paint job would hold up for ten years, but that was fourteen years ago. At present, the buildings are not even safe enough for painters to climb.

While researching the temple's history, I learned about some of the hard times it had experienced in the past. The main hall and priest's living quarters completely burned down in 1781, then again just four years later. Surely those buildings were still being reconstructed when they burned for the second time, painful as that is to imagine. The priest who must have stood there stunned, watching that awful scene, was named Daishin. The Akita clan chief who ruled the Miharu domain at the time took pity on him and purchased the nearby Sesson hermitage. The hermitage was transferred to create a residence for the priest, and that building is now the *shoin* reception room in the present-day living quarters. We hoped to leave that area unchanged and rebuild the rest of the living quarters.

Maintaining the temple for the future

After requesting some estimates, I found builders within Fukushima Prefecture to be incredibly expensive. Prices had gone up by over 50 percent what we had been quoted before the earthquake, showing the enormous impact of the reconstruction economy and Abenomics. That was not surprising given the labor shortage in the area, which was so extreme that contractors had to limit the jobs they took. Regardless, since I had no reason to believe prices would come down in the next few years, I decided my only choice was to start asking for donations.

I do so with a heavy heart. In all honesty, I wish we did not need to do any construction work at all. On further reflection, however, this feels like a mission that has been set before me. It has to be done, and the longer we put it off, the harder the job will become.

The Chinese character meaning "temple" (寺) originally meant "to retain in the same state." That character in turn is part of the characters for "samurai" (侍), "wait" (待つ), "to make a request" (恃む), and even "hemorrhoids" (痔), possibly because each are related to conditions that are difficult to change. In any case, maintaining a temple is a lot of hard work.

20
The Eight Winds

May 2014

In Japan, we have a name for the first wind of spring (as well as the second and beyond), and we describe the weather in late winter as "three days cold, four warm" as we impatiently await spring's arrival. Especially in northern Japan, we keep an eye on news reports of where the plum and cherry trees are blossoming as spring slowly creeps northward to greet us. Maybe this penchant for assigning numbers to such things is a sign of how much we look forward to them.

Where I live, pheasant's eye flowers and sasanqua blossoms create vivid patches of color in the snow at the end of winter. When the narcissus flowers bloom, we know spring is right around the corner. These flowers are smothered under a heavy blanket of white but manage to rise up nonetheless. I believe that is why the people of northeast Japan particularly love these cold-weather flowers, along with the fragrance of plum blossoms.

In February we had a particularly heavy snow that toppled the red plum tree in front of our main hall. Its limbs were already painted in scarlet buds, about to bloom. For a moment, I was reminded of the horror of the Tōhoku earthquake, but upon reflection I realized a "natural disaster" of this scale is just part of living in Japan.

Today, I would like to consider the wind.

The kanji character for "wind" (風) is a combination of a character for the mythical Chinese "fire bird" and one that today means "insect," but here indicates a dragon. The wind is a natural phenomenon driven by forces transcending human knowledge or control. Wind pollination takes advantage of this, and many plants rely on it to survive. The wind is possibly the aspect of nature that we most frequently encounter.

The Chinese philosopher Zhuangzi thought that the earth lived by wind, just as people breathe air. The wind benefits us in many ways, from drying our laundry to, more recently, producing electricity. We speak of metaphorical headwinds when forces seem to be against us, but with skillful maneuvering, we can turn these into tailwinds.

A Zen saying teaches us that the wise will not be carried away by any of the eight winds. This refers to the dangerous gusts of prosperity, decline, honor, disgrace, praise, censure, pleasure, and suffering. Prosperity and decline are both forms of unrest, and disgrace (criticism spoken behind our back) and censure (criticism spoken to us directly) both produce anger, so it is easy to see how these can upset us. Also, pleasure

Wind God

I come bringing spring

and suffering can both become clouds obscuring the moon if we do not know how to make the best out of both situations.

It is harder to see why we should avoid honor (being commended to our faces) and praise (being commended without our knowledge), but flattery throws our state of mind out of balance. We feel exultation when we learn that people are speaking well of us, and that wind can sweep us off our feet. This is not to say that Zen Buddhism teaches that we must avoid all emotions. Rather, we want our emotions to glide by us like a breeze, softly caressing us instead of blowing us away.

21

Chestnut Flowers

July 2014

I recently reread, for the first time in many years, *Narrow Road to the Deep North*, the travelogue that Matsuo Bashō (1644–1694) wrote late in life. Bashō is said to have practiced Zen meditation under the guidance of a Rinzai priest named Bucchō, making him a fellow Zen practitioner. It is also said that when he was living in the old province of Ōmi, he stayed at a hermitage called Genjū, which was named after a hermitage on China's Mt. Tianmu led by the Zen master Zhongfeng Mingben (1263–1323), where a priest named Kaizan associated with our temple went to study. Zhongfeng's teacher Gaofeng Yuanmiao (1238–1295) makes an appearance in *Narrow Road to the Deep North* under the name Priest Genmyō, confirming that we share the same school of Zen.

Be that as it may, I of course become most interested when Bashō's travels take him to the region that is now Fukushima Prefecture. "Approaching the Shirakawa Barrier [a frontier fortification in what is now the city of Shirakawa], I felt that our journey had truly begun," he writes, giving the impression that having come so far into Japan's interior, he can only continue down that narrow road. He recalls many old poems and admires how the whiteness of the *unohana* flowers and brambles alongside the road remain unchanged from when those poems were written.

"Pushing towards the north, I crossed the River Abukuma, and walked between the high mountains of Aizu [Mt. Bandai] on the left and the three villages of Iwaki, Sōma, and Miharu on the right, which were divided from the villages of Hitachi and Shimotsuke districts by a range of low mountains."* Under cloudy skies, Bashō can see all the way to the prefecture's borders to the west, east, and south. He ends up spending four or five days in the town of Sukagawa.

There, Bashō presents to a local poet named Tōkyū a haiku he wrote at the Shirakawa Barrier:

> *Deep in the country,*
> *a song sung when planting rice.*
> *The birth of fūryū [refinement, elegance].*

From this I read that the first time he encountered something like culture since departing on his trip was when he heard a rice-planting song somewhere near Shirakawa.

After that, he visits a reclusive monk who has made his home in the shade of a large chestnut tree near Sukagawa. Seeing how the monk lives, Bashō is reminded of the poet Saigyō (1118–1190), who lived off the acorns he gathered, and writes this haiku:

> *Chestnuts by the eaves—*
> *Why is it that we never*
> *notice their blossoms?*

One of the characteristics of Bashō's poems is that they often contain small discoveries like this. Here is another:

> *Look closely at the*
> *hedge there and you will see the*
> *shepherd's purse blooming.*

Again he mentions something that most people would overlook. Even his most famous haiku,

> *An old pond.*
> *A frog jumps in—*
> *the sound of the water.*

is a discovery of suddenly animated life against a backdrop of stillness.

In my humble opinion, the world of Zen is a world after loss. People naturally lose various things as they age, but in a Zen monastery, those things—information, friends, useful tools, and so on—are stripped from us at a much younger age. But we also awaken to a new set of values, one that remains valid even after loss.

It is now the rainy season, helping the chestnut trees quietly bloom. As evacuees from the earthquake and tsunami are forced into increasingly long stays in temporary housing, I hope that more residents of our prefecture will take note. Loss can quite effectively make people notice new things.

> *Oh summer grasses,*
> *standing in remembrance of*
> *the dreams of soldiers.*

It is nearly the season of "summer grasses," but if we think of the world after loss as a "remembrance of dreams," the thickly growing weeds come to look like a riot of dynamic life.

---

* Matsuo Bashō, *The Narrow Road to the Deep North and Other Travel Sketches* (New York: Penguin Books, 1966), 106.

22
Publishing Academic Papers

September 2014

On August 14, an academic paper on which I was listed as a coauthor was published in the British *Journal of Radiological Protection*. The primary author was Koike Takeshi, an associate professor with the Tohoku University Faculty of Science, writing on behalf of the Miharu Misho Project—the source of the data discussed in the paper. This project was established after the earthquake to help ease the minds of residents in the town of Miharu, and when a press conference was held about the study, my attendance was requested since I am the project's vice-representative.

There are various levels of involvement for coauthors of academic papers. In this case, the paper was written in English, so it was not easy for me to read through the versions that came back to me. Furthermore, the content was quite technical, so I suspect many people will give up on reading it partway through (like I did).

By the time of the press conference, however, I had managed to read a Japanese translation, so I thought I had gotten a grasp on its main points. According to my understanding, the gist was that by interpreting multiple post-earthquake materials, the authors had shown that tellurium-132 is an important factor in estimating exposure immedi-

THE SOCIETY FOR
RADIOLOGICAL
PROTECTION

The Miharu
Seedling Project

ately after a nuclear accident. They also showed that since the amount of released tellurium-132 has a fixed correlation to the amount of released cesium-137, total amounts of tellurium-132 can be estimated when cesium-137 values are known, with some exceptions.

Miharu was one of the only towns where the local government distributed iodine tablets to its residents after the nuclear disaster, and Dr. Koike also investigated the timing at which we took them. In addition, since children in the town wore OSL dosimeters from an early stage, he was able to forecast ten-year exposure doses from the measured values.

Having read this far, you can see that the primary academic findings of the study were the correlation between tellurium-132 and cesium-137, and the resulting ability to estimate radiation exposure immediately after a nuclear accident. The investigation into the timings at which iodine tablets were taken was secondary. Newspaper articles, however, did not mention tellurium at all. Their stories were all about the distribution and use of iodine tablets. Through this experience, I realized how difficult it can be for the mass media to cover scientific research.

Of course, explaining to the general public the issues that interest specialists after many years of study can be challenging. Even so, when media outlets detect some hint of newsworthiness, their job is to report (what they perceive to be) an overview of the research to the public.

You might wonder why I became coauthor of a paper that was so easily misunderstood by reporters, despite my not even being a specialist in its field. The only reason I can give is because Dr. Koike asked me to and I trusted him. I once asked him what he thought when a certain scientist accused of fabricating data publicly stated that she had performed successful experiments "over two hundred times," and he flatly stated, "She's even sloppy in the way she's defending herself—if she's performed successful experiments 213 times, or 227 times, she should know that, and say so."

If that very sober outlook strikes a chord with you, please take a look at his paper. You can read it at the Miharu Misho Project website (http://iopscience.iop.org/article/10.1088/0952-4746/34/3/675).

23

The New "Dream Island" Concept

October 2014

One of the things I worry about these days is what will happen to the towns and villages in Fukushima Prefecture's Futaba District, one of the districts closest to the destroyed nuclear power plant. It has been three and a half years since the nuclear accident, yet some 120,000 former residents prefecture-wide remain unable to return to their homes. They are forced to live in temporary housing, some within and some outside of the prefecture. Many have started putting down roots in their new homes, so it is unclear whether it will be possible to reboot administrative functions in the Futaba District.

A similar thing happened after the nuclear accident in Chernobyl. Several villages were abandoned, but two years later, a new town called Slavutych arose to take their place. A new birth through merger, if you will. This new city was built 50 kilometers east of the accident site. Radiation at ground level was dangerously high at first, but it was lowered by replacing the ground surface with uncontaminated soil. High-rise apartments and single-family homes were built, with occupancy preferentially offered to disaster victims. The town offered an excellent environment for welfare and education, and so today has attracted a population of about 25,000 people, including those who are not disaster victims.

As a Reconstruction Design Council member, I proposed the creation of such a town as a new home for disaster victims in Japan. I thought the national land along the southern side of Lake Inawashiro might be a good candidate for this town, or the national forest in the western part of the city of Iwaki, but honestly even I was unsure whether former residents of the coastal Hamadōri region could acclimate to the cold. In the end, the council did not take up my idea as a proposal, and it was disbanded shortly afterward, so I lost my forum for making such grand plans.

A new town would involve nearly every governmental ministry, so the council would have been important as a way of transcending the boundaries between ministries and agencies. However, the government bureaucrats behind the council were not allowed to provide it with any input, and today I cannot help but think this extreme exclusion of the very people who would be implementing whatever decisions the council made led to their abandoning it altogether.

Despite the time that has passed, my dreams of creating a new town have not subsided. Reading Naka Yukiteru's book *Fukushima genpatsu: Aru gijutsusha no shōgen* (The Fukushima Nuclear Disaster: A Technician's Testimony; Kobunsha, 2014) has further fueled these dreams for our own birth through merger.

Naka proposes that we use rubble from the disaster to create an artificial island off the coast of the Futaba District, upon which we can build research facilities and residences. High-rise buildings would limit the effects of radiation on residents. The artificial island beneath Kansai International Airport could provide a technological model, putting the project within the abilities of Japanese engineering—notwithstanding some differences between the Seto Inland Sea (site of the airport) and the Pacific Ocean (proposed site of the new community).

As I have discussed before, Japan has progressed from building earthquake-resistant five-storied pagodas to the Tokyo Skytree. Isn't it time we took a similar step forward with an eye to mitigating tsunami? Naka's proposal strikes me as a dream that should encourage us all. In fact, it reminds me of a television show I loved as a child titled "Hyokkori hyōtan-jima" (The Madcap Island). Wouldn't it be wonderful to see a "dream island" unexpectedly appear off the coast of the Futaba District?

24

The "Fukushima 50"

November 2014

When a tsunami wiped out electricity at the Fukushima Daiichi Nuclear Power Plant, about six thousand employees were on site. Of those, approximately two thousand were working within the restricted areas around the six reactors. Units 5 and 6 were in "cold shutdown" for periodic maintenance. Units 1 through 4 were operational, however (with Unit 4 partially disassembled for maintenance), so loss of power meant an inability to cool the nuclear fuel rods within those reactors, threatening a meltdown that would release large amounts of radioactive material.

Starting in the afternoon of March 12, the day after the tsunami, a series of hydrogen explosions occurred in Unit 1. I sometimes think about how terrifying it must have been to be working at the plant at that time. Some contractors and subcontractors evacuated their employees. Some employees had lost homes in the tsunami and left to search for their families. In the end, only the late Yoshida Masao, the plant manager at the time, and a few hundred employees remained on-site to try to get the situation under control. According to the testimony Yoshida delivered to a government investigative committee, he was worried that all of Eastern Japan might become uninhabitable.

The Guardian quotes manager Yoshizawa Atsufumi as saying, "We felt like members of the Tokkōtai [the special attack unit of kamikaze pilots during World War II] in that we were prepared to sacrifice everything. . . . No one was forced to stay, but those of us who remained knew that we would be there until the end. We knew that we were the only people capable of saving the plant. Our determination surpassed all other considerations."

The self-sacrificing efforts by him and his coworkers saved Eastern Japan, possibly even the world. During this period, they were unable to bathe, had nothing to eat but snacks and dried foods, and had to sleep on hard floors. Yoshizawa described how the poor diet and sleep deprivation took a toll on his health, resulting in weight loss and soaring blood pressure.

American media outlets like ABC News and the *New York Times* quickly named these workers the "Fukushima 50," and their story spread to other international media. I am not sure where the "50" comes from, since there were hundreds who remained, but regardless, they went largely unrecognized in Japan. Despite being counted among the "heroes of Fukushima" when awarded Spain's Prince of Asturias Award for

Concord, Tokyo Electric Power Company (TEPCO) employees were not included among the representatives of Japan's Self-Defense Forces, National Police Agency, and Fire and Disaster Management Agency who went to accept the prize.

Possibly a general consensus that TEPCO was to blame for the accident resulted in pressure not to recognize any of its employees as heroes. I can see a case being made for that attitude, but still—failure to reward the selfless efforts of those individuals diminishes the heroics that took place in the disaster area. Personally, I would like to momentarily set aside the problems that remain with organizations such as the Japanese government and TEPCO and once again thank those brave workers who acted so courageously during the disaster and continue doing so today.*

---

* This essay borrows extensively from the following *Guardian* article: https://www.theguardian.com/environment/2013/jan/11/fukushima-50-kamikaze-pilots-sacrifice

25
The Virtue of Forgetting

January 2015

In Japan, we hold *bōnenkai*, or "forget the year" parties in December, followed by New Year parties in January. While we tend to be fond of celebrations in general, I consider this sequence of forgetting followed by renewal to be particularly Japanese.

I have heard of Chinese people seeing the characters we use to write *bōnenkai* (忘年会) and assuming it must be an event where we drop formalities related to age (because "age" is another possible meaning for "year"). A *bōnenkai* is indeed an informal affair—and that interpretation is not far from the original meaning of the word, as described below—but what we hope to forget with today's custom is not our age but the suffering we have experienced during the past year.

Come to think of it, Japanese greetings tend to emphasize the present while forgetting even the immediate past: "good day" in Japanese (*konnichiwa*) is literally "this day," dissociating it from yesterday, and our "good evening" (*konbanwa*) is "this evening," a separation from the afternoon that preceded it. This sounds to me like an attempt to always be starting something anew. The predecessor of *konnichiwa* appeared as *konnitta* in the Muromachi era (1336–1573), so these greetings that imply starting over from the beginning have been around for some half a millennium.

At just around that time, Prince Sadafusa (Gosukō; 1372–1456), who would later become a Buddhist priest, wrote in his diary about a year-end gathering for reciting poetry. There, participants would drink a cup of saké then recite one hundred verses of *renga* poetry. Everyone of course got more and more intoxicated as the night went on, leading to what the prince described as such a fun time that everyone forgot how old they were. This was the first mention of such an event in literature. Eventually, commoners also took up the custom of holding "forget your age" parties. The only difference between those year-end parties and our own is that we no longer recite poetry. In any event, the custom of *bōnenkai* clearly goes way, way back.

I often hear the opinion that the Japanese cannot constructively move forward with plans because they forget things too often. However, diversion from our daily suffering may be highly meaningful and important for the mental health of ourselves and those around us.

I often encounter people fretting that their memories of the Tōhoku earthquake and tsunami seem to be eroding or fading away, but I cannot see how such a thoroughly learned lesson could be so easily forgotten. If anything about those days is forgotten, I can only imagine it is so trivial or painful as to warrant being lost.

People sometimes experience a state in which they are unable to proceed without forgetting something. Perhaps we have some subconscious mechanism for selecting matters that should be forgotten and erasing them from our memory. This allows us to enjoy the benefits of a natural sifting process that retains only the things important enough to learn and remember. This is a behavior specific to humans that no computer can emulate.

In the end, the things we forget by attending a "forget the year party" are things we would naturally fail to remember anyway. Rather than being careful not to forget things, it is better to actively try to forget anything extraneous. By forgetting that all things come to an end, we can remember the joy of new beginnings.

I wish a truly happy New Year to all of you.

26
Symbiosis

February 2015

Somewhere near the ocean that gave birth to life in the distant past, prokaryotic cells, the direct ancestors of humankind, encountered the foreign organisms we today call mitochondria. These organisms were foreign in that prokaryotic cells shun oxygen and perform repeated cell division, whereas mitochondria love oxygen and almost never divide. At around this time, oxygen levels in the atmosphere reached about 2 percent, making it difficult for anaerobic prokaryotic cells to survive

in isolation. Faced with no other option, they combined to coexist as eukaryotic cells. This symbiotic theory was so far removed from Darwinian "survival of the fittest" that it was a long time before academia accepted it.

However, a similar phenomenon also occurs in cultural matters, one example being the assimilation of Buddhism into Japan. With the incursion of the foreign organism known as "the Buddha," the native *kami* (gods) had to reform so they could coexist in a competing state. This is similar to how conventional prokaryotic cells formed a nuclear envelope and tried to protect genetic information when merging with mitochondria.

My dwelling on such matters is likely a result of the terrorist incident that occurred in Paris on 7 January 2015. On that day, two French Algerian brothers forced their way into the offices of the satirical newspaper *Charlie Hebdo*, where the staff were in the middle of an editorial meeting, and killed the editor-in-chief and eleven others. Not only France but many countries immediately condemned this act, accelerating anti-terrorism measures. It goes without saying that such violence threatens freedom of expression and the press itself, and can never be forgiven. However, if we carefully consider the background against which such incidents occur, it seems unlikely that the problem can be fundamentally solved by forcibly "eradicating terrorism."

In 2004, as part of a broad movement to ban conspicuous religious symbols, France forbade Islamic women from wearing the hijab in public schools, and then most public places in 2011. I suppose they had every right to do so, but one can see how these acts would be humiliating to followers of Islam. The newspaper that was targeted in this particular event was known for its political cartoons, but Islamic society discourages the creation of any pictures depicting actual living subjects such as people and animals, calling this an imitation of God's act of creation.

This is why Arabic art developed as arabesques and geometric patterns. But *Charlie Hebdo* had gone even farther, breaking the powerful Islamic taboo against depicting images of Muhammad (multiple times, and in highly provocative ways), making them a target for Islamic extremists.

Radicals like those who attacked *Charlie Hebdo* are by no means representative of Islamic society, but if that society continues to be misunderstood, radicals will continue to emerge. There have even been cases of Japanese being taken hostage and executed. But I believe the essence of the matter, or rather the increasingly clichéd logic of the game, lies in the artificial "survival of the fittest" concept that is globalism.

There are approximately 1.8 billion followers of Islam in the world. Over 60 percent of them live in the Asia-Pacific region, but more than 43 million live in Europe and the United States.

Today we cannot survive without mitochondria, so I wish I could ask them what scheme they used to achieve their symbiosis. Or perhaps it is the prokaryotic cells who know . . .

27
Okinawan Graves

March 2015

In early February, I went to the main island of Okinawa to give a talk. Every time I visit Okinawa, I cannot help but be impressed by the graves there. Everywhere I go, I see graves in the "turtleback tomb" style that arrived some eight hundred years ago via China's Fujian and Yunnan provinces, the *hafu-baka* style with their characteristic roofs, and the *horikomi-baka* graves built into natural cliffs. These graves are amazing in part for their size, but also because they were designed not for individuals or families but for an extended patrilineal lineage known as *monchū*.

Large-scale graves require large-scale maintenance. This maintenance is commonly performed during leap years in Okinawa, with the families involved making donations to pay for it. Some large graves even have stone plaques with family names and donation amounts carved into them. I saw some with clearly Western names, showing how the family spread throughout its history. Many listed twenty or thirty different family names from Okinawa, the mainland, and beyond.

I was told that when unmarried women or children age seven or younger die, their remains are interred to the side of the gravesite for a time, then placed in a funerary shrine with the remains of another person who died at a later date. Perhaps this is another example of Okinawan respect for procreation and family connections.

Visiting Yachimun ("Pottery") Street in the Okinawan capital of Naha, you will see many large, colorful funerary urns for sale. Those who die at age eighty or older are considered to have lived out their natural life span, and the custom even today is for grandchildren to purchase and gift the urns that will hold their grandparents' remains.

Until the 1950s, the custom in Okinawa was to leave bodies in a cave until they were reduced to bones, which were then ceremonially washed and placed in an urn. Today, however, most people are cremated. On the thirty-third anniversary of death, the deceased's bones are removed from their ornate urn and buried within the soil of the funerary shrine. An offering of a pig's head and tail (or, even better, the entire pig) is made, and the family enjoys a celebratory meal.

I was surprised to learn that in this way, ancestors' remains are not just tucked away somewhere, but cared for long after death. Okinawans also have multiple opportunities other than annual memorial services to have meals at gravesites. What better way to foster a sense of "returning" to the resting place of the *monchū* grave?

Oh! Our family grave!

Overall, we Japanese tend to refer to the post-death state using the phrase "that world" in place of "the Pure Land" or "heaven," possibly to foster a sense of returning to a familiar place. On the mainland in recent years, however, graves have increasingly become places for individuals and single families, reducing their role of evoking nostalgic memories.

When leaving home on the mainland, we announce, "I'm going and I'll be back," but I understand that there is no equivalent in the Okinawan dialect. Rather, the expression used there presumes the speaker's return, so there is no need to explicitly state it.

Okinawa has had the highest birthrate in Japan for forty years running, and I cannot help but wonder if the promise of *monchū* and the Okinawan manner of handling death have something to do with that. Here on the mainland, where birth rates are declining, I believe we will soon be entering an era in which each gravesite will have to be maintained by at least two or three families. Okinawa will remain a place of nostalgia, and one with an exciting future.

28
Soft Stone?

April 2015

There are people in the world whose lives are profoundly shaped by happenstance. I met just such a person the other day in the city of Numazu in Shizuoka Prefecture.

The day after giving a talk at the Hakuin Forum, an event commemorating the Numazu-born Zen master Hakuin Ekaku (1686–1769), I visited the temple of my cousin Sōitsu there. He is a stonecutter as well as a priest, and standing before the enormous collection of carvings outside his temple, I found myself somewhat overwhelmed.

Sōitsu is the eldest son of my father's older brother, and I have known him to be an odd sort ever since he trained at the Engakuji Temple monastery in Kamakura. Once when I was a child and he was still a novice monk, he came to stay at my family's temple during the Obon holiday. One evening he retired to sit alone in meditation. He remained completely motionless even when I entered the room, making him somehow unapproachable. I noticed that many mosquitos had gathered on his wrinkled robes, and I could hear the whining buzz of their wings. Drawing nearer, I saw a swarm of the insects arise like black smoke from his arms, face, and head. "Isn't that itchy?" I asked. "Of course it is," was his matter-of-fact answer. What a peculiar man, I thought.

Some time passed during which we did not meet, but I heard he had learned to play the shakuhachi flute and had even become an instructor. He ended up joining a temple affiliated with Hakuin, and every time I see him nowadays, he is eager to talk about Hakuin and stone-cutting.

He told me he had met a very interesting stonecutter who had given him the stones that were now scattered throughout the grounds of his temple. Sōitsu would carve Zen expressions, haiku, and sutras into their polished surfaces, and recently he had been carving tracings of Hakuin's calligraphy. His collection is becoming quite large.

"Stone is soft," he once said. While seemingly a contradiction, I suppose you can scratch stone with a single nail, so perhaps there is something to that. But still, stone to me is hard and cold. When he told me he polishes natural stone not with sandpaper or files but with his bare hands, at first I could not believe it.

Eventually, however, I recalled the story of the dexterous butcher from the "Essentials for Nurturing Life" chapter in the ancient Chinese text *Zhuangzi*. A skilled butcher, it says, faces an ox with his spirit, not his eyes, allowing the knife to follow the natural form of the animal, carving rhythmically without ever hitting bone. The butcher in the story relates that he has used the same knife for over nineteen years, carving up thousands of oxen.

I gathered up the courage to ask Sōitsu how frequently he had to sharpen his chisel. He told me that he only uses a rounded chisel, and he had not sharpened it for five years. Apparently, if you use the chisel correctly, the act of carving stone itself sharpens the tool. I was impressed. Cousin though he may be, I was forced to reappraise Sōitsu as the master craftsman he had become. The priest's robes he was wearing made me imagine him as Mokujiki (1718–1810) or Enkū (1632–1695), both renowned for their sculptures.

Isn't
that
itchy?

Of course
it is.

The year after next will mark the 250th anniversary of Hakuin's death, and there will be a ceremony that has been held once every fifty years since. Sōitsu tells me he has been asked to create a memorial stone that will stand at the site of Hakuin's birth. Through a curious series of coincidences, his life continues to proceed in unexpected directions.

29

One-*mon* Prayers

May 2015

The repairs to the main hall at our temple that started last May are proceeding well. The roof is now mostly sheathed in copper, and it was quite a thrill to see the gleaming plating when the protective sheets were removed on April 10. The cherry blossoms on the temple grounds were in bloom, putting flowers and metal in a competition to see which could be more brilliant.

Takahashi, the head of the carpenters working for the construction firm Katō Kōshō Co., Ltd., called it "the most beautiful of scenes," but something about that shiny copper plating sets me on edge. As-is, the roof does not blend well with the scenery in Japan, but I am sure he was already envisioning the more subdued color it will eventually become.

Just one month before, the bases of several support pillars resting on the foundation stones of the main hall were cut away to splice in new ones. In the more than two hundred years since they had first been placed, three of the pillars had started to rot and needed to be reinforced. When performing that task, the carpenters from Katō Kōshō were surprised to find the bottoms of the pillars were discolored with a curious green. Upon inspection, they discovered oxidized *Kan'ei tsūhō* coins that had been placed between the pillar bases and the foundation stones. According to the three carpenters, there were likely coins under each of the seventy-plus surrounding supports. At first, we were just surprised, having no idea why the original builders would do such a thing, but looking closer we realized that only the discolored areas remained untouched by rot. It was impossible not to be impressed by our ancestors' knowledge and wisdom.

A local carpenter told me that copper plates are still inserted beneath support pillars to prevent termite infestation. I have also heard that if you immerse a copper plate in a pond where spirogyra is growing, the water will become clearer before your eyes. Whatever is in that bluish-green substance that comes from copper, it apparently has insect repellent and antiseptic effects.

Doing a little research, I learned that *Kan'ei tsūhō* coins were made not only from copper, but also from brass and iron. The most valuable coins were made of brass, usually with those having four waves drawn on the back being worth four *mon* (the unit of currency in Japan until 1891), and others being worth one.

While it is not a huge amount of money, it is fun to think of the hoard of coins hidden beneath the pillars of our main hall. Rather than

being just a copper plate, I feel as if these little coins are also like little prayers.

When the repairs were complete, I asked the carpenters what they had done with the coins they had found.

"We left them embedded in the pillars, where we found them," they said.

"Well then, what's between the foundation and the bases you spliced in?"

"We inserted fifty- and five-yen coins."

"You . . . what?!"

While I can see that it might be difficult to procure replacement *Kan'ei tsūhō* coins, fifty-yen coins are made of cupronickel, and five-yen coins of brass, so I am doubtful we will get the same effect.

Takahashi told me he had considered also inserting pieces of copper plate, but he decided to use only coins because he was concerned about compatibility between the metals. I will leave it to the people a couple hundred years from now to find out whether we achieved the result we were after.

30

Carpenter Bees vs. Carpenters

June 2015

Last month, the repairs to the roof over our main hall were completed, but this has in turn led to all kinds of unexpected work. The first task not accounted for among the originally planned design and construction work was cleaning up all the civet droppings. A family of masked palm civets has been living in the eaves of our main hall for some years. Until now, they had primarily made their presence known through the pattering of little feet during nighttime meditation sessions, but now we had to deal with several years' worth of their accumulated feces.

Civets are omnivores, and their droppings included many ginkgo nut shells, undoubtedly from the large ginkgo tree that stands in our graveyard. There were so many shells that I figured they must have stockpiled the nuts as their primary food source in winter, when other sustenance would be scarce. In any case, their excrement was layered so thick it took the carpenters several days to get rid of it all.

After that, the carpenters' work seemed to be progressing smoothly. It was not long, however, before we encountered another unexpected snag: my wife noticed an uncommonly large number of holes that carpenter bees had drilled into the eave supports between the rafters and the roof. This posed yet another difficulty following the one just solved,

Carpenter bee

Carpenter♥

Palm civet

and another unexpected task to take care of.

Carpenter bees—in our case, *Xylocopa appendiculata*—are generally not interested in humans. The males do not have stingers, and the females will not attack unless provoked. Even if one does sting, it usually is not a big deal. I often saw them sipping the nectar of wisteria flowers, but had never been particularly troubled by them; they were just a subject for quiet contemplation. But this! It felt like a betrayal.

It just so happens that a couple who were bee specialists visited us at around that time. According to them, carpenter bees love to drill holes in the rafters of wooden buildings, where they store the nectar and pollen they collect. They also build many small nests in these holes, where they lay their eggs and feed little balls of nectar and pollen to their young. It is from all this building activity that they get their name. All this happened just as the wisteria I had transplanted from up in the mountains over twenty years ago came into full bloom. Wisteria relies on carpenter bees for pollination, so it is good at attracting a lot of them. The bees also seemed to like our peonies.

Fixing all the damage they had done by drilling those holes would be a lot of extra work for the carpenters. But Takahashi is a master craftsman, and having noticed the damage the carpenter bees had done, he felt unable to ignore it. Thus began a war of carpenter bees versus carpenters, the former focused on the maintenance of their home and brood, the latter on plugging up the former's holes one after another. The two sides fought for a week in the idyllic battlefield that is our temple grounds.

I express my sincerest thanks to the three carpenters—Takahashi, Okuyama, and Itō—for what they described as the most perfect filling job they had ever performed. I can only hope for their fine work to last for so long, however; the carpenter bees have already changed the target of their affections from the wisteria to the flowering black locust trees around here, and the buzzing of their wings has not abated as they busily work through their year-long lifespans.

31
Kawauchi and Rhododendrons

July 2015

In early June, I gave a talk in the village of Kawauchi, which like my temple is in Fukushima Prefecture. This was just before the start of the rainy season, and white flowers stood out in the mountainous landscape. The contrast between the greens of planted rice paddies and the white flowers of the dogwoods was beautiful, making the journey of about ninety minutes by car seem short.

Kawauchi is famous (among some) as the location of Tenzan Bunko, the house where poet Kusano Shinpei (1903–1988) wrote many of his works, and as the natural habitat of the Forest Green Treefrog, known locally as the Kinugasa flying frog. It became known more broadly throughout Japan when the Tōhoku earthquake struck and the resulting nuclear meltdown led to the evacuation of the entire village. Many likely still recall the tears of Mayor Endō Yūkō when announcing the evacuation, and I was very happy when his was the first of the eight villages in the Futaba District to announce it was safe to return.

Before the earthquake, Kawauchi had a population of a little over 2,900 people. Of those, only 1,800 have returned. Some have relocated to larger cities within the prefecture, but over 400 are living outside the prefecture.

In his New Year's address this year, posted on the Kawauchi Village website, Mayor Endō wrote that "recovery is a matter of perseverance and staying power." He promised to "work hard to create an environment that will allow everyone to return to their former lives whenever they consider it the best time to do so." I think those words do an excellent job of conveying the mayor's own perseverance and staying power, as well as his strength in not giving up. The gap between his gentle demeanor and his strength of spirit is very admirable. His is the strength of softness.

In the entranceway to the Kawauchi town hall, there is a ceramic frog figurine carved with the words "return safely" (the words for "return" and "frog" are homophones in Japanese). It represents the town mascot, a Kinugasa flying frog named Moritarō. I could not help but laugh when I saw it, because it reminded me so much of Mayor Endō.

I suspect that his parents named him after Hamaguchi Yūkō* (Osachi), the twenty-seventh prime minister of Japan. He was a man of such conviction and principle that he continued to perform his duties in the Diet even after being shot in an attempted assassination, saying that people should not be inconvenienced on his account; in doing so, he likely shortened his life.

Given the chance to meet the mayor on this trip, I had intended to share how the prime minister's name was actually the result of an accident. When his father, having drunk too much after learning he had a son, went to the town hall to register his birth, he mistakenly listed his name as the unconventional "Yūkō," rather than the intended and much more common "Yukio." I hoped to convey that unlike Hamaguchi, he should look after himself, but unfortunately the mayor was in Tokyo on some reconstruction-related matter, so I was unable to meet with him.

There has been progress in the area. A solar power company is moving in, traditional village wells are being dug, and medical facilities are

Kawauchi

being established. The Fukkōmai brand of rice, developed as an economic revitalization measure, is delicious, and the cultivated acreage for rice and buckwheat has increased. The village has many accomplishments to report, including follow-up decontamination procedures following completion of primary decontamination, but what moved me most was the joyous announcement by Education Superintendent Akimoto Masashi of the children selected to perform the traditional lion dance.

Also memorable was the beauty of the rhododendrons blooming in the garden at Tenzan Bunko. They go beyond simple flowers: their countless blossoms glitter overhead as if they themselves were the sky seen through dappled sunlight, creating the most brilliant display of floral beauty that I have ever seen.

---

* Hamaguchi's given name was Osachi, but the characters can also be read as Yūkō, which became the name by which he was popularly known. When the characters for Yūkō (雄幸) are reversed, the name can be read as Yukio (幸雄).

32

The Power of Resolve

August 2015

The other day, Kyoto University's Kokoro Research Center hosted a cross-disciplinary symposium on the Tōhoku earthquake and tsunami. The theme was "Toward a rebirth of the spirit."

I gave a talk describing the ambiguity of the concept of *mono no aware* (an awareness of transience and impermanence) that was popular in the Heian period and how it can be viewed as an impactful amalgamation of joy and sorrow. Indeed, the word *aware* was used so frequently at the time that its meaning became vague and emotion-based, requiring people to surmise its intended meaning according to context. This is not unlike how "kawaii" is used to refer to nearly anything today.

Apparently taking exception to the situation, the warrior-turned-monk Saigyō (1118–1190) wrote the following poem:

> *To think I found*
> *The moon poignant*
> *In the capital—*
> *What a trifling pleasure*
> *It now seems.* *

He seems to be saying, in a quite scornful way, that describing the moon as evoking *mono no aware* is nothing but a meaningless way (a "trifling pleasure") for urbanites living separate from nature to pass the time. Warriors, who tended to disdain vagueness in language, eventually came to consider *aware* only in negative terms, and started using *appare* ("praiseworthiness") instead. In my talk, I hoped to present Fukushima Prefecture as a mixture of *aware* and *appare*, but with the latter not being as apparent as one might hope.

At the symposium, I found the presentation by Inoue Vimala of Koyasan University particularly interesting. In a quite timely talk titled "From the Perspectives of Mindfulness and Resilience," he spoke about a taiko drumming group that Koyasan helped reestablish in the tsunami disaster zone. Through the concept of the "rebirth of the spirit," he was able to draw on the classical power of religion while still presenting a discussion pertinent to modern times.

In a later email, we discussed *adhiṣṭhāna*, which he interprets as including the meaning of resolve. In Japanese, *adhiṣṭhāna* is translated as *kaji*, a term most often used in the compound *kaji-kitō*, or "ceremonial blessings." This may evoke an image of superstition in some, but in fact, the *ji* in *kaji* means "to retain mental focus," while the *ka* means "the bestowal of transcendental forces that occurs as a result"—something that is only likely to happen through a high degree of resolve. In this literal sense of the word, most works of art are the product of at least some *kaji*-like force. Our discussion of moving "toward a rebirth of the spirit" thus took us to the core of both art and religion.

---

* Robert Sewell, "The Path of the Poet-Priest Saigyō," *Denver Quarterly* 12, no. 2 (1977): 120–126.

33

The Linear Precipitation Zone

On September 10 and 11, oddly corresponding with the anniversary of a certain international calamity, the northern Kantō and Tōhoku regions were hit with unprecedented rainfall. Floods and landslides occurred in Ibaraki, Tochigi, Fukushima, Miyagi, Yamagata, and other prefectures, causing deaths and forcing many residents to evacuate. Many rice paddies nearly ready for harvest also suffered disastrous damage.

September, called the "long month" in the old Japanese calendar, is a month of long rains even in normal times, but this year some locations saw more than twice their normal monthly rainfall in just one day. Although typhoons are usually followed by much-welcomed clear skies, in this case such expectations went unfulfilled—the rain clouds just refused to move on.

This apparently happened due to a "cold vortex" of −9°C air in the upper atmosphere that merged with the moist air of Tropical Storm Etau, which had transitioned into an extratropical cyclone, and Typhoon Kilo, which was moving north from the east. The Japan Meteorological Agency calls the resulting phenomenon, in which rain clouds continually and intensively occur in an area about 200 kilometers wide and 500 kilometers long, a "linear precipitation zone." There was talk of something called the Madden-Julian Oscillation as well, but whatever the cause, abnormal weather is definitely increasing worldwide these days.

Meanwhile, people are raising concerns about the ground's reduced ability to absorb water. Many civil engineering works, such as pavement and concrete-lined drainage ditches, postpone the absorption of rain into the ground, carrying it from where it fell to some other distant location. But so much water is now being diverted in this way that rivers cannot accommodate it all. Concrete-lined ditches and stone walls also block air and water from passing through soil, causing the soil to lose its absorptive ability and thus its resiliency, making it vulnerable to erosion in heavy rainfall.

Actually, after the Obon holiday, I had a specialist come to assess the water and air permeability of the soil in our temple grounds and graveyard, and to take measures to improve it. He used a device he called an "air shovel" to create ditches, into which he placed things like scrap charcoal, bamboo, tree branches, and leaves. These ditches were not particularly deep, but he told me they promoted air permeability and the growth of soil bacteria, which would gradually restore the soil's health.

When he showed me what he had found, I noticed a clear relation between weakened trees and the condition of the soil in which their roots were growing. Places where our cherry trees were withered or had diseased branches were near soil that had been hardened by a concrete surface, or stone walls that were built without consideration for drainage. The very next day, I was surprised to see new buds in place of sick leaves on trees in areas where he had performed his restorative soil treatments. The large trees growing here now draw stagnant air out of the ground and pull fresh air in; even after those long rains of September, the treated areas of our temple grounds and cemetery looked refreshed, not waterlogged, by the downpour.

The town where I live is on the eastern edge of the linear precipitation zone that developed last month. The heavy rains did not last as long here as in places where there was severe damage, making them an opportunity to give thanks for our good fortune, as well as to reconsider our relationship with the very ground we walk on.

34

The Nanto Rinzankai

November 2015

I have recently visited the city of Nara nearly every year. This started with a trip right after I finished my novel *Ashura* (Kodansha, 2009). It just so happened that the Tokyo National Museum had hosted the *National Treasure Ashura and Masterpieces from Kōfukuji* exhibition that year, so thinking it might be best to get advance permission to publish my novel, I sent the manuscript to Tagawa Shun'ei, the head priest at Kōfukuji Temple in Nara. He sent me an immediate reply by letter, writing, "As a fellow follower of the Buddha, I trust you."

After that, I received one invitation after another, first to give a talk at the Nanto Nirokukai (a consortium of Buddhist temples in Nara), then at an event hosted by Nara Toyota . . . I just can't seem to stay away from the place.

Every time I visit, I come to like that ancient city even more. Nara is famous for its deer, reminiscent of the Indian city of Sarnath. I was surprised to learn that the deer in Nara originally came from Kashima Shrine in Ibaraki Prefecture, and even more surprised to learn that there is such a thing as "deer jail." It seems that once deer learn the taste of human crops, there is no going back, and they become repeat offenders. If caught, they are sent to the slammer—a life sentence. I asked whether any are ever offered amnesty, such as upon the appointment of a new chief priest, but apparently that does not happen.

Anyway, this year I visited Nara again, on November 9. I had been invited by a group called the Nanto Rinzankai, a fellowship of six temples in and around Nara: Tōdaiji, Kōfukuji, Saidaiji, Tōshōdaiji, Yakushiji, and Hōryūji. I was meeting with them at Tōdaiji to receive donations they had collected for a relief fund I direct, the Tamakiharu Fukushima Fund, which supports young Fukushima refugees. They were also donating to Japan Earthquake and Tsunami Orphans, a nonprofit organization from Miyagi Prefecture, and the Nara Chapter of the Japanese Red Cross Society. The gathering included the chief priest of each temple, along with their deputies, deacons, and other dignitaries. The autumn foliage was at its peak, and the scenes of deer against brilliant red leaves on the Tōdaiji grounds made me feel like I was inside a classical painting.

We held a ceremony in the Great Buddha Hall of Tōdaiji, and Tsutsui Kanshō, the administrative head priest there, conducted a ceremony to confer the donations as well. The whole time, we were surrounded by a crowd of tourists who had come to see and photograph and worship the

Great Buddha. We in turn were seated on a stage just above the seated Vairocana Buddha's thighs. I very much enjoyed myself, knowing I would likely never experience anything like it again.

The vestments worn by Nanto clergy are called *kegyō-kesa* or *tasuki-kesa*, with the cord hung on the left shoulder and a sash hanging down to the right. I think they make those wearing them look quite intellectual and active, possibly because the Nanto Buddhists are such erudite scholars.

There, in the Nara of late autumn, amidst this finely dressed assembly, I vowed to continue my activities with the Tamakiharu Fukushima Fund.

35
Losing Is Winning

February 2016

From the end of the previous year through the start of this one, it has been a very mild, snowless winter. Red plums have bloomed since year-end, and even the *fuki* (butterbur) sprouts have begun to appear.

When we find ourselves in a situation like this, we tend to say things like "I don't expect this to hold," or "The cold's just building up, I bet." We expect things to eventually balance out, that bad must come with good. "Good luck and bad luck are intertwined," the Japanese saying goes, and it seems an apt description of how we view the transitions of nature. It is a sound way of thinking, well suited to this post-disaster period of reconstruction. But nature's variability follows no rules. We may end up getting no snow at all this winter, or we might experience record snowfall. Nature tends to defy expectations.

The Japanese have come up with another curious saying: "To lose is to win." This does not mean that losing now will allow winning later, nor does it imply that loss becomes the foundation for future victories. It simply states that losing is itself winning, a sentiment that on its face makes little sense. I recall reading somewhere that while most Japanese sayings have at least a rough equivalent in Western languages, this one is the exception—the concept just does not exist in the West.

The reason why losing is winning is because loss invokes an instantaneous change in values. You have lost according to some measure, sure, but you can immediately apply a new value set by which the experience would have been a win. In a sense, it is evidence of a life lived without a fixed set of values. In other words, it seems as if there is in the world a sort of defiant spirit saying it is better to lose than to live by the values thrust upon it.

It is possible I am thinking about such things because of a woman whose funeral I conducted the other day. Kiyoko was born deaf and passed away at the age of eighty-nine. In her case, rebelliousness did not really enter the picture, but she definitely lived a life of values differing from the norm. Unable to hear the voices of others or even her own, she had developed "Kiyoko-speak," a unique set of gestures and utterances she used to communicate with those around her.

After she died, I assigned her the dharma name Ten'niin, which might be translated as something like "heavenly ears," along with Aikyō ("love and respect"), for the emotions she evoked in others. Finally, I also named her Jōfuku ("purity and good fortune") to retain the meaning of "Kiyo" from her given name. I think this properly describes a life in which "losing is winning."

36
Myōhō

April 2016

Five years after the Tōhoku earthquake and tsunami, I recall the words of the monk Ryōkan Taigu (1758–1831). The following is the closing of a letter he sent inquiring after a friend, Yamada Tokō, a victim of the Sanjō earthquake of 1828 in what is now Niigata Prefecture:

> When the time comes to meet with disaster, we should
>   meet with disaster.
> When the time comes to die, we should die.
> This is the *myōhō* [supreme dharma] by which we escape
>   disaster.

Tokō, a saké distiller who was friends with Ryōkan through their shared interest in poetry, survived the earthquake uninjured but lost a child. Judging from these words, written right after the disaster, the two must have been quite close.

In the first half of the letter, Ryōkan remarks on how bad the earthquake was, but writes that thankfully his hermitage was undamaged and that no one close to him was killed. He also includes a poem:

It is a far greater misery to survive the sudden loss of so
    many
Than to have joined them in their passing.

While I am sure this reflects Ryōkan's state of mind to some extent, my guess is that Tokō felt it far more deeply, having lost a child. What Ryōkan is writing about is yielding to nature while remaining compassionate for human suffering, as described in the ancient Chinese text *Zhuangzi*. It is a state of quiet faith in the inexorable forces of nature.

I also recalled the words of Holocaust survivor Viktor Frankl (1905–1997), who challenged us to celebrate our destiny and trust in its significance. Having survived the human disaster of Nazism and its concentration camps, Frankl relentlessly sought meaning in life. Unsurprisingly, he refused to accept that his experience had anything whatsoever to do with "nature." The branch of psychotherapy he developed, known as logotherapy, is based on the belief that people can resolve their mental problems by discovering the meaning of their own lives (*logos*). Even having lost his parents, brother, and wife in concentration camps, he bequeathed to us this important way of thinking that tells us to say "yes" to life.

I presume that many victims of the Tōhoku earthquake—even those who over the past five years have started to accept the disaster that took their homes and families as another aspect of nature—have wavered back and forth over whether they can truly say "yes" to their lives as survivors. I suspect that the different views of Ryōkan and Frankl are due not only to differences between Japan and the West, but also to the differences between natural and human disasters.

Especially in Fukushima Prefecture, where a high number of disaster-related deaths were caused in part by human actions, people are searching for meaning in their post-disaster lives. Unlike Nazism, which

history has fully repudiated, nuclear power is still not completely viewed as a mistake, and plans to restart Japan's nuclear power plants remain underway. This has obscured the meaning in the deaths of those we lost in the disaster, along with the meaning of life for those who survived.

Our national government has promised psychological care for disaster victims, but if it were sincere in that intention, its first step would be to decommission the Fukushima Daini Nuclear Power Plant, rather than leaving the decision up to its operators.* As part of that decommissioning, they must also settle upon a final disposal site for spent nuclear fuel. Even if they do not quite attain *myōhō*, I urge them to strive to find meaning in the deaths and lives of so many people.

---

*On 31 July 2019, TEPCO announced that it would close all four reactors at the Fukushima plant.

37
Big Data

May 2016

A poem by Liu Xiyi (c. 651–680) says "flowers bloom the same way year after year, but people are never the same." In truth, however, flowers can change too. For example, this year, when I went walking through the hills behind our temple to view the cherry blossoms, I noticed countless flowers on a weeping cherry tree that had never bloomed before. I planted that tree right after returning to this temple from my training as a monk, thirty years ago. Every other tree I planted has blossomed beautifully during that time, but this one alone would instead grow a full load of leaves when it was supposed to be flowering, so I assumed it was somehow sick. I had planted it too close to the other cherry trees anyway, so if it did not bloom this year, I was considering that I might have to cut it down.

As if reading my thoughts, the tree underwent a remarkable transformation. The saying goes that "If you haven't seen a boy for three days, you're sure to find a difference," but this was the first truly big difference I had found in this particular lad in three decades.

In our graveyard are two other cherry trees that at one point had been near death but had bounced back remarkably last year after we opened holes in the surrounding soil using a tool called an air shovel.

I saw new shoots on their branches the very next day, thanks to the improved air and water permeability. One of the reasons for my flower-viewing walk was to check on these trees, and sure enough, all their branches were covered in blossoms. A truly impressive recovery. One is a type of weeping cherry called *Edo higan*, and the other is an ordinary *Somei Yoshino* cherry. I could not say what was going on inside of those trees, but whatever it was, it was remarkable.

Seeing such changes in trees made me want to shift my attention to the human world. In his poem, Liu Xiyi laments that the girl he looked at flowers with so long ago is no longer with him. People are always changing, and that change includes aging, sickness, and death.

Flowers look different to us while we are sick compared to when we have recovered. Or perhaps it is because the flowers look different that we can say the viewer has changed. In other words, isn't this poem an expression of a strong emotion resulting from an insistence that flowers should be the same every year?

I have heard the national government intends to start collecting and using a form of anonymized medical information that it calls "big data." Apparently, the plan is to create an institution that will collect data on

the results of various therapies and health examinations, without the consent of the persons that data came from. The stated goal is to develop new drugs and therapies, but I am a little worried about how else the data might be used. Plus, tracking numbers of illnesses and symptoms is fine if it will somehow advance drugs and therapies for them, but what about rare and difficult-to-treat illnesses?

The other day, I conducted a funeral for a temple parishioner who died due to an illness called "progressive supranuclear palsy," which I understand affects only one in a million people. That means there are only around one hundred patients with this disease in all of Japan. No known therapies or cures exist for this affliction, so my parishioner met a truly piteous end. I certainly hope that "big data" will be applied in some way unrelated to market economics, so that such people can undergo a transformative experience like that of the two cherry trees at my temple.

38

Asa (Morning)

June 2016

Two days ago, a member of one of my parishioner's families died. Her name was Asa, which means "morning" in Japanese. Coming up with a dharma name for her got me thinking about mornings.

To begin with, the pronunciation of *asa* is well suited to the Japanese morning, a sound that makes you suddenly open your eyes and mouth. Possibly it is the "s" sound that makes me feel the wind. Since long ago, morning in Japan has started with folding futons, or hanging them outside to dry. The power and movement of the wind keeps us from lounging about in bed all day, and it is right there in the pronunciation of *asa*. Come to think of it, the NHK morning drama for 2015–2016 was titled *Asa ga kita* (Here Comes Asa!), and I understand it had very high ratings. I wonder if its title had something to do with that.

By contrast, the English word "morning" sounds somehow sleepy to me, possibly because it is a homophone with "mourning." It feels as if it still will not be completely awake for a while, so we should just leave it be.

The kanji for *asa* is also used in many compound words with meanings related to government. Researching this, I learned that in China's Shang dynasty (c. 1600–1046 BCE), all important governmental matters were decided at early-morning meetings that began at dawn, and this established the connection between morning and government. From what I understand, governmental affairs at the imperial capitals of Nara (during the eighth century) and Kyoto (from the eighth to nineteenth centuries) started at dawn and ended at noon.

The Chinese philosopher Zhuangzi uses a word that includes the "morning" character to describe a state similar to Buddhist enlightenment, making me wonder if morning was viewed as having some sort of spiritual power.

In my own case, I find that my imagination runs wild at night, making it easier for me to write, but I never submit those manuscripts as-is. I wait until I have had a chance to reread them in the morning, when the clearer air puts my thoughts in order. The result is usually many corrections.

Not everything is good in the morning, however. For example, my phone rang at six thirty this morning, and whenever I get a call at that time, my first thought is that somebody must have died. Sure enough,

that is what had happened. This time, the caller was an old classmate who now works as a hospital pharmacist. Through tears, she told me that her father had passed away.

She has always been the type to wear her heart on her sleeve, so her tears were not particularly surprising, but I had a deep sense that her crying was more profound than I had expected. When she later came to the temple to officially notify us of her father's death, she explained the situation: her father had passed just when she had momentarily left his side, and she felt so guilty about it she had not slept at all.

The hospital proclaimed his death at 11:50 p.m. When she came to the temple with her husband, her eyes were still bloodshot. From this I learned that the power of Japan's morning relies on a good sleep the night before. Regardless, every morning that passes helps to lessen our grief.

39

Resilience and *Kotobuki*

July 2016

I gave a talk at the Japanese Society of Anti-Aging Medicine's sixteenth conference held the other day at Pacific Convention Plaza Yokohama. Thumbing through the thick program they sent me, the word "resilience" stood out. As I paused to wonder why that word sounded so familiar, I realized I had come across it when reading up on psychiatry for my book *Ashura*.

Like "stress," the word "resilience" originally came from physics. While stress refers to distortion due to an external force, resilience is a force that corrects distortion, or in some cases resists it in the first place. Another definition is "an ability to maintain equilibrium even in extremely unfavorable situations." Indeed, unfavorable situations cause different amounts of stress in different individuals. Those who experience less of it have a certain obstinacy of spirit, which is what psychology and psychiatry call resilience.

When I heard about anti-aging medicine, my initial response was that it is pointless to resist aging. The phrase takes on a very different nuance, however, if you read the "anti-" as a form of resilience—it seems to indicate a bright, positive attitude that does not concern itself with aging.

Mimura Masaru, a professor in the Department of Neuropsychiatry at the Keio University School of Medicine, asked me to give a talk about my book *Shiawaseru chikara* (The Power to Create Happiness; Kadokawa, 2010). Just knowing how the Japanese word for happiness, *shiawase*, originated and changed is enough to increase our mental resilience, he said.

In that book, I showed how the Japanese word for happiness originally referred to a more passive responsiveness, and how its intuitive responsiveness was historically enhanced. If we are to make a direct connection with anti-aging, however, we have to talk about *kotobuki*, a word with a variety of meanings, including "celebration," "congratulations," and "longevity." The kanji used to write *kotobuki* originally meant "long life," making it a single-character description of longevity. In that case, the Japanese thought, it is important to express congratulations in words, or *kotohogi*, a word that eventually morphed into the *kotobuki* reading that today is assigned to the longevity kanji.

Being born as a boy or as a girl, living in a certain town, finding an occupation and someone to live with . . . these are all happy things, things to celebrate. The Japanese mindset is that if you start by celebrating the situation you find yourself in, then regardless of whether it rains, or you have an accident, or an earthquake occurs, or you get cancer, you can still find something to be thankful for. You can consider yourself as having gotten off lightly, and you can use calamity as an opportunity for reconsidering your life. In this worldview, good and bad emotions are not considered equal; liking is viewed as a skill, but disliking is nothing more than desire. While there are limits, our resilience is well supported by the word *kotobuki*.

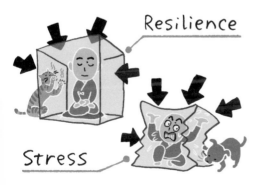

Resilience

Stress

40

Faint Crescent Moon

August 2016

For some reason, July reminds me of the Three Mountains of Dewa. While I have only been there once, my memories of the place remain vivid. The three mountains—Yudono, Gassan, and Haguro—each have distinctive features, and since ancient times, they have been a site of a mixed Shintō and Buddhist practice that is hard to describe in simple terms. At least, it is hard to describe now that the two religions are less interwoven than they once were; perhaps such a harmony of beliefs was the norm in ancient times.

Taking advantage of a regional lecture series in the area, I went on a three-day, two-night bus tour there. I always enjoy trips like that, but on this trip, everything I saw and heard was just incredible.

The red earth of Yudono left a particularly strong impression on me. I was surprised when a person in white robes like those of a Shintō priest appeared and started chanting the Buddhist Heart Sutra. He was even carrying something similar to the wands Shintō priests use in their rituals, but he called it a *bonten* (a name derived from Brahma [Jp. Bonten], an originally Hindu god that Buddhism has adopted). Perhaps it is because I have been sullied by modern thinking that I wanted more clarification of what was Shintō and what was Buddhist. Instead, I felt as if a previously firm footing was crumbling beneath me.

Later, a guide led us up a mountain trail where snow still remained. While I would have liked to pause and contemplate the contrast of summer skies overhead and snow beneath my feet, I had to remain focused on learning from my swiftly moving guide the knack of walking along the boulder-strewn path.

"Think of each rock as a monk's bald head," he said. "If you step on the wrong place you'll snap his neck, but each one is telling you where to step. Just do as they say."

Not the kindest of advice, I thought, but I found that by focusing on following his instructions, my body naturally took over and performed a sort of dance down the trail. The distance of every stride and the angle at which I placed my foot made every step different, defying the formation of patterns in my gait and forcing continued concentration.

When we finally reached the top of Mt. Gassan, my guide gave me a piece of paper cut into a human form. He told me to touch it to any part of my body that was not feeling well, then place it in a nearby stream.

"That's from Taoism!" I thought, my face revealing my revelation. He replied with an impish grin as if to ask, "Have you got a problem with Taoism?"

As we descended toward the Haguro Shrine, we came across an astoundingly magnificent five-storied pagoda standing in the middle of the dense forest. I could not help but wonder how on earth its builders had managed to haul the building materials up here, but I was already so overwhelmed by wonder that my head was spinning.

That night, we stayed at the temple lodgings for pilgrims where our guide lived. It was a Shingon Buddhist temple, so I laughed a little when I saw it was decorated with statues of snakes and various gods.

It was a fun night, like being on a school field trip. The crescent moon outside the restroom window reminded me of a haiku by Bashō:

How cool it is here—
A crescent moon faintly hovers
*Over Mount Haguro.**

I am quite fond of the "faintness" of that crescent moon. It contrasts with the starkness of our segregation of Shintō gods and Buddhist deities, as well as Buddhism and Taoism, since modern times have ripped them apart.

For whatever reason, I was in top form for at least ten days after that trip. Maybe it was from stepping on all those monks' heads, or perhaps it was a blessing from a faint crescent moon.

---

* Matsuo Bashō, *Eibun shūroku: Oku no hosomichi* [The Narrow Road to Oku, Bilingual Edition], trans. Donald Keene (Tokyo: Kodansha, 2007), 116.

41
Wasan and Sangaku

October 2016

In Miharu, the town where I live, there has recently been a lot of talk about *wasan* and *sangaku*. *Wasan* is a uniquely Japanese form of mathematics developed during the Edo period (1603–1867), and *sangaku* are geometry and other mathematical problems written on small wooden tablets and given as offerings to shrines or temples.

People sometimes donated *sangaku* depicting difficult problems they had thought up themselves, while others used them to issue a challenge to rivals. In a sense, shrines and temples thus became intellectual battle-grounds. Perhaps it was this type of intellectual exchange, which took people beyond their typical roles, that laid the groundwork for Miharu to become a center in the Freedom and People's Rights Movement of the Meiji era (1868–1912).

Seki Takakazu (1642–1708) is known as one of the founders of *wasan*, and he makes an appearance in Ubukata Tow's novel *Tenchi meisatsu* (Discerning the Universe; Kadokawa, 2009), which I enjoyed very much. But a *wasan* slightly different from Seki's developed in the Tōhoku region. Central to that development was Sakuma Yōken (1819–1896), who taught *wasan* at Meitokudō, a school in the old Miharu Domain.

While most of the more than two thousand students he taught were the children of samurai, among them were also the children of farmers and merchants. In his classroom, they would set aside social rank and class as they sought solutions to difficult *wasan* problems. After completing their work, the farmers and merchants would walk the several *ri* (1 *ri* being about 4 kilometers) home from Sakuma's school, then return again the following morning. I cannot help but wonder where such enthusiasm comes from.

Many *sangaku* have been found in the shrines and temples of my town. Here is an example problem found at Miharu's Itsukushima Shrine in 2009:

You have a snake, 10 *shaku* long. When it curls in on itself and touches the middle of its belly with its nose, what is the diameter of the circle it forms? (Use 3.16 as π.)

There are many pictures drawn on the shrine's latticed ceiling, but I imagine no one expected the one depicting an enormous snake wrapped around cherry blossoms and the trunk of a pine tree to be part of a math problem. After the problem, the answer is written on the plaque, along with "Watanabe Ichirō [from] Aza Furuuchi." Having solved this difficult problem, Watanabe likely hired someone to make this *sangaku*, which he used both to thank the gods for their aid and let the world know of his accomplishment.

The snake *sangaku* was dedicated in 1885, the eighteenth year of the Meiji era. The Imperial Diet would not be established for another five years, but at the end of 1885, the first Itō Hirobumi parliamentary cabinet was formed. Other notable events that year included massive flooding in the Kansai region that washed away almost all the bridges in Osaka, and the Convention of Tientsin, a result of the Japan-backed

Gapsin Coup aiming at Korean independence from the Qing dynasty.

There are many similarities between the then-and-now of natural disasters and the state of Japan's relationships with its closest neighbors. Today, however, we seem to lack the academic fervor of that earlier era, which had ignited during Japan's *sakoku* (closed-borders) era and was still smoldering in 1885.

Seki-school *wasan* was very popular in the Iwate Prefecture town of Ichinoseki, whose local lord had been transferred from Miharu. Perhaps the academic passion there was related to the movement of people within an isolated country. Regardless, my hope for today is that we can all enjoy enough peace and security to engage in pastimes like *wasan*.

42
Desmostylus

December 2016

The other day I went to Hokkaido for the first time in a long while. I was visiting Honbetsu, a small town around three hours east of Sapporo. At least, its population is small; by land area, it is quite large. In fact, its neighboring town Ashoro is one of the largest towns in Japan by land area, amazingly only slightly smaller than Kagawa Prefecture. Honbetsu is much smaller than that, but even so, it is about the same size as Nagoya.

I was invited there through a connection with Sueh Toshimitsu, whom I know because we are both judges in the Letter from Mother to Child contest. Sueh is a former NHK newscaster who got his start at the Obihiro Broadcasting Station and now performs as a storyteller under the stage name Kanda Kōyō. He also teaches volunteers at the Honbetsu Library techniques for reading out loud, and he introduced me to a seminar sponsored by the library.

Honbetsu grows delicious soybeans and uses them to make outstanding miso, *nattō*, and sweets. Local businesses also serve locally raised beef and wine produced in the nearby town of Ikeda. It was already late October when I visited, but we were blessed with good weather nonetheless, and despite having to give two talks, I had a very relaxing time. Two things in particular stand out from my trip: the fact that Honbetsu was the source of warhorses used by the Imperial Japanese Army, and the *Desmostylus* that is the title of this essay.

Most Japanese warhorses were bred and trained in Honbetsu but never returned from war. A museum next to the library exhibits information about those horses and Baron Nishi Takeichi (1902–1945), a gold medalist at the 1932 Los Angeles Olympics in equestrian show jumping who was also involved in horse training as a member of the Tokachi Warhorse Replenishment Division. The photographs that I saw there of horses killed in the war were as shocking as the thunderstorm I experienced on the third day of my visit, but I would rather not go into the details of either. The odd creature that sits in front of the museum is far better material for stoking the imagination.

Desmostylus was an aquatic mammal that lived in the sea back when Hokkaido was divided into several parts by the ocean (or rather, before the multiple islands that formed Hokkaido had merged). Even a young specimen was 1.8 meters long, and they could grow to some 300 kilograms. Their skulls have also been found in Gifu Prefecture, and they seem to have once been quite populous along Pacific coasts in the

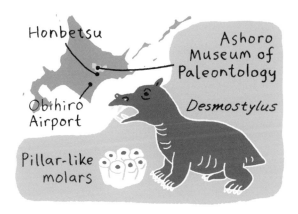

Honbetsu

Ashoro
Museum of
Paleontology

Obihiro
Airport

Desmostylus

Pillar-like
molars

northern hemisphere, including those of Japan. The name comes from the Greek words for "bound" (*desmos*) and "pillar" (*stulos*), a reference to the structure of the pillar-like teeth they likely used to graze on seaweed and other plants.

I visited the Ashoro Museum of Paleontology, where a curator who was enthusiastically researching these beasts gave me detailed descriptions. Also on display was a fascinating skeletal model of *Ashoroa*, an ancestor of *Desmostylus* that is named after the town.

It is interesting to consider why we have hippos and sea turtles today, while *Desmostylus* went extinct. I do not expect that seals or sea lions gave them many problems, but maybe walruses were too much for them? Thinking along those lines, *Desmostylus* starts to seem like a creature that was too awkward and gentle to exist in this world.

43

The Ink of Kobaien

January 2017

The other day, Nara Toyota invited me to give a talk, which gave me an opportunity to visit Nara during the busy month of December. Every time I am invited to one of these events, Nara Toyota president Kikuchi Osamu plans a local sightseeing trip for me for the following day. In previous excursions, I have visited places I otherwise would only rarely be able to see, including Tōdaiji, Saidaiji, Mt. Shigi, Kinpusenji in Nara's Yoshino District, and Tsubosakadera. These were wonderful experiences, very different from an ordinary visit, because I was being shown the very heart of these places.

This time, I enjoyed a rather extravagant tour of the Tōshōdaiji and Yakushiji temples, but before that, we visited Kobaien, a famous shop that has been making *sumi* ink since the sixteenth century. I am sure nearly all calligraphers in Japan would recognize that name. Our guide was the sixteenth-generation president, Matsui Shōko.

The factory grounds cover approximately 2,300 square meters, with two light-rail lines conveying the flat dollies used to transport in-process and completed ink sticks to where they need to be. Matsui guided us through each of the production steps in turn. I knew that ink sticks are made from soot, aromatics, and a binding agent, but I was a little surprised to see the extent to which the company adhered to traditional production methods.

The first room we visited was a dim space where vegetable oils from sources such as rapeseed, sesame, and pine are put into earthen pots and burned, using wicks woven from rush pith to collect the soot. She told us that workers turn the pots every twenty minutes so that the soot is distributed evenly within. Countless flames flickered in the darkness, where two workers were engaged in the difficult task of maintaining the pots.

We next visited the room where aromatics such as borneol and musk are kneaded into the soot and binding agent. I was even allowed to try my hand at it, producing a semisolid ink stick. The sticks are then washed and dried for a few days, resulting in the finished product.

We then proceeded to the drying room, which was also amazing to see. The ink sticks are first covered in damp ash to prevent them from drying too quickly. This is later replaced with dry ash, and finally, the sticks are carefully hung in straw to dry naturally. Each of these steps is performed by an experienced craftsperson.

"Each task is handled by a specific person?" I asked.

"That's right," Matsui replied.

"I guess somebody taking a sick day would really mess things up, then."

"It does," she said, explaining how hard things are for everyone when an employee catches a cold. From the perspective of "resilience," which I have discussed before, this does not sound like an optimal system. But even so, I could not help but be impressed by the tightrope walk that this operation has been performing for so long.

It may have possibly been my extreme surprise that caused me to lose my business card holder somewhere along the path of our tour. I was stuck without it during my visits to the Tōshōdaiji and Yakushiji, but

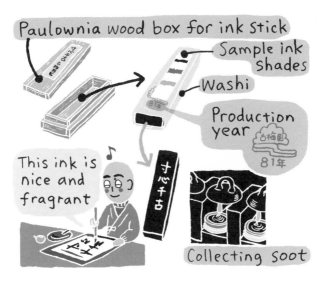

when I arrived back at Nara Toyota at the end of the day, it had already been delivered to me there, along with a stick of the finest pine-soot ink. Someone told me that Matsui herself had delivered it, leaving me even more impressed with the kind of individualized work that defies system-ization. I will certainly be buying my ink from Kobaien in the future!

44

Soil and Buildings

February 2017

The other day, we held this year's first planning meeting about construction on the living quarters at my temple. Maeda Shinji, chief architect at Kurashijisshoku Architects Office, usually travels from his office in Ise to attend these meetings around once a month, and he made the long trip here.

This month's meeting was also attended by many others, including the on-site director from contractor Katō Kōshō, who always leads the meeting, and electricians, pump operators, foundation layers, and others who would be working on the foundation. Currently, the residence has been temporarily raised two meters off the ground, and a new foundation will soon be laid underneath it. At this meeting, however, we decided to take a somewhat different approach than usual.

Yano Tomonori of the consulting company Mori-no-Engei drew everyone's attention when he arrived around five minutes late. Yano is a soil specialist, and my wife and I were hoping he would win over the others with his ideas.

At the risk of oversimplification, Yano considers earth to be a living thing, and uses various methods to help it breathe. In the precincts of ordinary gardens as well as shrines and temples, he digs deep ditches connected to water veins and covers the bottoms of these ditches with charcoal, bamboo, soil, dead branches, and fallen leaves. By doing so, he creates sturdy ventilation routes like those in the natural world, which will not collapse even when stepped on. In an earlier essay, I described the work he did to revive the cherry trees in our graveyard, but this time we wanted him to apply the same strategy to the building's foundation. In both cases, we were talking about revitalization of weakened earth, a problem that is occurring on a global scale.

The common practice in the civil engineering and construction industry is to create a "mat foundation" by digging soil, spreading a layer of crushed stone, laying reinforcing bars on it, and then covering it all with a thick layer of concrete. While this method produces a stiff, strong foundation, it pays no consideration to the earth beneath it. Piles can be driven to increase the soil's firmness, but otherwise the soil itself is ignored.

Yano's position is that if the ground is unable to breathe, it will eventually die. In our case, there is a pond near the residence, so ideally the ground will allow air to pass through, but not water. He also wants to

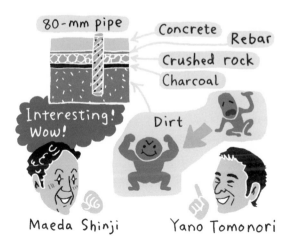

141

create surrounding passageways so that the groundwater does not become stagnant. If water does not stagnate and air can pass through, aerobic bacteria will propagate, the soil will be revitalized, and its load resistance will increase.

My wife and I watched Yano's presentation to the others with trepidation, wondering if he would be able to convince them to adopt his point of view. This kind of perspective on soil probably does not exist in the logic of the civil engineering world. As it turned out, however, we had nothing to worry about. Maeda, the designer, started out by saying, "Well now, that's quite interesting! Quite interesting!" He seemed to want to give it a try, even if it was a first. His enthusiasm was infectious, convincing even the foundation-layer who would be at the head of this endeavor. He said he would spread charcoal beneath the crushed rock and insert 80-millimeter pipes vertically into the concrete at intervals of several meters. "If everyone is behind this and we all work together, I'm sure it will go well!" he announced brightly.

After our meeting, Yano took us all to look underneath the residence, which had been built in the traditional manner with posts resting on individual stones set in the earth and the floor elevated above the ground. He used a shovel to dig away some of the old topsoil there. A single scrape was enough to reveal the brightly colored soil beneath the dull surface. He stood the shovel upright, and we were all surprised at how soft that soil was.

"This is ideal soil," Yano said, "permeable by air but not by water." Maeda once again exclaimed "Very interesting!" causing me to foresee a bright future for Japanese architecture.

Now an eight-ton truck is parked in the garden in front of the residence, where we have only just finished ground improvements. It seems a little early to subject it to such harsh treatment, but I suppose I will just trust in the strength of our revitalized soil.

45

"Oh Vreneli"

March 2017

The other day, I helped to organize a concert of Japanese musicians living in Switzerland. The main organizer was the Tamakiharu Fukushima Fund (http://www.osyf.or.jp), which I chair, and our sponsors included the Swiss Embassy and the Cabinet Office of Japan. Performers included alto singer Kutsuzawa Hitomi, pianist Iwai Yoshiko, and guitarist Nishishita Kōtarō, along with the Tachibana High School Orchestra from the city of Fukushima and the chorus from a local elementary and junior high school. It turns out that Tachibana High School's orchestra director Fukase Kōichi went to college with Kutsuzawa, helping to make the concert that much grander. The event was titled "A Concert to Support Fukushima Reconstruction: Together with Switzerland."

Indeed, we received many donations from Switzerland following the Tōhoku earthquake and tsunami, apparently a result of international media coverage. I myself recall being interviewed by television stations from France, Germany, Switzerland, and China. French and German are both official languages of Switzerland, so many German and French programs are also broadcast in Switzerland. This means the Swiss were able to watch not only their own domestic coverage of the Fukushima disaster, but also that of two other countries.

The relationship between Japan and Switzerland goes back much further, however. Most Japanese are familiar with the traditional Swiss song "Oh Vreneli," which Osaka YMCA director Matsuda Minoru translated into Japanese in 1949. While its melody is upbeat and bouncy, its lyrics as they were translated into Japanese are quite serious. "Oh, Vreneli," comes the call, "where's your home?" The response: "My home is in Switzerland, next to a beautiful lake." The second verse asks, "Oh, Vreneli, what is your job?" "I'm a shepherdess," she replies, but "I'm afraid a wolf will come."

I suspect that to postwar Japanese, the "wolf" was the kind of criminal that frequented black markets. The same year the song was translated, physicist Yukawa Hideki (1907–1981) became the first Japanese Nobel Prize recipient, but this was also the year of the Matsukawa derailment incident (sabotage of a railway passenger line by parties who remain a mystery to this day) and other events that left Japanese society on edge. I suspect that the merry yodeling in "Oh Vreneli" was cheerful encouragement to those still struggling to find housing and work.

When I hear this song in today's Fukushima Prefecture, I am tempted to replace "Switzerland" with "Futaba," as I am sure the nearly 80,000 people here who remain unable to return to their homes would do.

Where's your home? In the Futaba District, next to the sea. Where's your heart? Far away, beyond the mountains, in my hometown of Futaba.

Possibly feeling that the song did not have enough purpose, the University of Tokyo's Onkan choral studies group later added more lyrics: "Oh Vreneli, look at these arms! I'll chase away those wolves, to build a better future for Switzerland (Futaba)! Yo ho ho, tra la la la . . . Oh Vreneli, look! Follow in the footsteps of those rising up in the name of freedom for Switzerland (Futaba)! Yo ho ho, tra la la la . . ."

I wonder what the "wolf" is today for those living in the Futaba District, or other parts of Fukushima Prefecture? Nuclear power plants? Ignorant teachers who turn out the classroom lights and claim there cannot be too much radiation, since nobody is glowing? Both, I suppose. In that case, chasing away all the wolves will be no easy task.

In any case, the wonderful thing about our concert was not only the encouragement we received from the Swiss people, but our children and youth showing us the strength of their arms, and the footsteps they will follow as they rise up in the name of freedom. From beginning to end, this unsung song rang throughout me.

46
Gekka hyōjin

April 2017

I was recently asked to play the role of matchmaker. Young people these days have turned away from relying on help from matchmakers or shrines and temples to find a spouse, preferring to handle things on their own, but it is a different story when the groom is the assistant chief priest of a temple.

I often wonder whether the reason people today so easily decide to divorce is because it is so easy to get married. When marriage becomes a matter of simply filling in a form, divorce becomes simply filling in another one. I accepted the request because the man I would be playing matchmaker for was a young priest I thought well of, and I wanted to be able to extend my heartfelt congratulations to the young couple. When a matchmaker is involved, separating becomes far more difficult, and even though it was not really my business, I even went so far as to think of adding one or more weighty, irreversible elements to make it a wise marriage.

The *gekka hyōjin* that is the title of this essay is something of a digression. I already knew that matchmakers were sometimes called *gekka hyōjin*, but I did not know why. The kanji read something like "ice person beneath the moon," which does not exactly evoke warmth and emotion, so why would this idiom be applied to someone trying to help others come together?

There are various theories on the topic, and it is difficult to say which is correct, but one that makes sense to me is that *gekka hyōjin* is a combined form of *Gekka Rō* ("the old person under the moon") and *Hyōjōjin* ("the person on the ice"), both of whom are figures from Chinese mythology related to finding a spouse.

"The person on the ice" refers to a story in the *Book of Jin* (648) in which Suodan, a fortune teller, interprets a dream of a man standing on ice and speaking with someone beneath the ice. Above the ice is *yang*, he says, and below the ice is *yin*, so this dream portends the dreamer's success as a matchmaker who brings together *yin* and *yang*, the joining of which occurs when the ice has melted. In the story, the man does indeed go on to become a successful matchmaker, but I cannot help wonder, what is the ice?

I suppose the idea is that the metaphorical ice separating a man and a woman will eventually melt, but before that happens, the matchmaker must scurry back and forth between them. The biggest barrier blocking marriage is what the two do not know about each other (the unmelted

ice), so while that ice remains, it is important for the matchmaker to make an all-out effort to warm things up, so to speak.

Turning to the "beneath the moon" part, I read this as "until night-time." Specifically, my image is that one's activities as a matchmaker last until the moon comes out. Or perhaps the matchmaker borrows the mysterious powers of the moon?

The "old person under the moon" refers to Yue Lao, a god of marriage who uses a red cord to bind together couples who are destined to marry, long before they actually do so. According to legend, he appears at night, beneath the moon.

Putting this all together, *gekka hyōjin* is a person who works even until nighttime, utilizing the power of the moon to melt the ice between two people who do not know each other well, with the aim of getting them to marry. This does not at all describe me.

The Chinese *Shijing* (Classic of Poetry) contains a verse that says, in essence, "Young man, if you wish to take a woman for your wife, do so in winter, before the ice melts!" All this thinking about irrelevant things has led me to see the importance of what is not yet understood (covered in ice).

Perhaps a marriage comes to an end when one spouse thinks they have fully "understood" the other. Maybe it is what we do not understand about others that makes them attractive, and knowing that we do not understand everything that makes us humble.

San-san-kudo ("three-three-nine times") is a part of traditional Japanese wedding ceremonies in which the bride and groom exchange oaths involving multiplication of three by itself to obtain nine, which signifies "eternity." The threefold and ninefold prostrations that we monks perform have a similar meaning, eternal devotion. Perhaps not understanding provides the path toward eternity in both devotion and marriage.

47

The Children's Parade

May 2017

May 5 is Children's Day in Japan, and every year in my town of Miharu, we hold a parade on that day, a tradition dating to the Taishō era (1912–1926). This year we were blessed with good weather, allowing us to enjoy an idyllic, fun, and peaceful event.

Small children in the parade are viewed as children of the Buddha, and we pray for their health and growth. They wear opulent costumes that are probably based on the clothing of nobility in the Heian era (794–1185). A flagbearer carrying a multicolored banner leads the parade, followed by a white papier-mâché elephant riding on a wheeled base, then behind that, a leader wearing a classical *kamishimo* outfit who guides the children. Parents hold the hands of very young children, who wear hats and crowns based on Heian-era court fashion.

While we hold this event annually, the group of children is of course different each year, so they must gather the day before to learn how to wear their costumes and perform in the parade. This year we had many children between the ages of three and five, so it was quite difficult, with some refusing to leave their mothers' arms and others running about wildly.

We gather early on the day of the event, leaving time to inflate the balloons we pass out to those watching from the roadside. We are joined by women wearing *kappōgi* smocks who will serve *amacha* (a sweetened herbal tea) to visitors. Members of the Miharu Buddhist Society use a truck to fetch the (quite remarkable) papier-mâché elephant from the warehouse it is normally stored in.

Elephants are sacred animals in India, where the Buddha's mother Māyā is said to have learned she was pregnant when she dreamed about a white elephant. This is why elephants in children's parades are white. We went elephant-less for a couple of decades due to war, but after that, monks at local temples collected alms to help fund a new one, which was created by woodworkers. At the start of the Heisei era (1989–2019), we had it professionally repaired and repainted. It is designed so that a child can sit beneath its belly and beat a drum. The base is painted like a blue sky with white clouds.

The old saying goes that people who ride in a palanquin depend on those who carry it and those who make the carriers' shoes, and while this event is, in simple terms, just children dressing up and walking down the street, preparations for it require the hard work of many people. Children are indeed our future, and we will make whatever efforts are necessary.

When the Children's Parade resumed after the war, over one hundred children participated each year. Today it is more like twenty. Meanwhile, our elephant is aging, in the sense that the men in charge of pulling it every year are getting older.

A bakery owner who has helped with this event for many years once suggested that we someday bring an actual elephant, and this subject comes up every time the preparation committee gets together for drinks. We speculate about how much a circus would charge us for elephant rental services and so on, but nothing ever comes of it. I imagine we would draw quite a crowd if we had a real elephant walking down the street, but then the elephant, not the children, would become the star of the show. We would also have to increase our security, with police and everything, so we would lose something of the normal tranquility, and that tranquility is what I consider to be the best part of this event.

For whatever reason, each year I am assigned the task of painting a silver-white line down the noses of children who have finished changing into their costumes. I must say, I have become quite the expert at tracing down children's noses. I sit in a chair and the children, accompanied by their parents, stand in front of me. Some wait with their eyes open, others closed, but what is interesting is how that simple silvery-white streak seems to instantly envelop them in the special aura of the festival.

We all gather for a commemorative photo beneath the gates at the former site of the Meitoku Domain school, then finally set off on our walk. Of course, we are traveling at the speed of three-year-olds, so the pace is leisurely, to say the least—an unhurried tempo symbolic of peace. By the time we have reached the temple and wrapped things up, most of the children will have lost the streak down their nose, but even this is a lesson from the Buddha about impermanence.

48

The Utility of the Adam's Apple

July 2017

An ever-increasing number of people are dying from aspiration pneumonia. For many years, cancer was the leading cause of death in Japan, followed by heart disease and stroke, but in 2011 pneumonia rose from fourth to third place and has remained there ever since. In fact, the direct cause of death even in cancer patients is often pneumonia, so its true rank may be even higher.

Microorganisms that can cause pneumonia are present in the mouths of even healthy people. Aspiration pneumonia results from accidentally inhaling bacteria-laden food, which causes it to enter the lungs through the trachea. This happens because the laryngeal muscles that surround the Adam's apple weaken, causing them to sink lower and make it harder for the epiglottis to close.

If you think about it, the throat is a busy place, as we use it to breathe, swallow, and speak. When we swallow, the epiglottis immediately closes off the passageway leading from the nose to the lungs. This happens in just half a second, and if that timing is even a little bit off, the result can be pulmonary aspiration—that is, foreign matter entering the airway. Therefore it is important to strengthen the laryngeal muscles, but how can we do that? I recently read a book called *Haien ga iya nara, nodo o kitae nasai* (If You Don't Want to Catch Pneumonia, Train Your Throat; Asuka Shinsha, 2017) by Nishiyama Kōichirō, which tells us exactly how.

The first step is something called the "Shaker technique," which I had heard of before. When you lay down in bed at night, take away your pillow and lift your head until you can see the tips of your toes. Hold that position for a minute or so, at which point your neck will likely be quivering. This is a good lesson in how little we exercise our necks.

Next is the "forehead exercise," where you press the palm of one hand against your forehead as hard as you can, as if they are fighting each other, maintaining that state for a few seconds. This is best done while sitting at a desk or a table.

The last part is the "chin-raising exercise." Here, you place the thumbs of both hands under your chin and press your thumbs up and chin down with the same force for a few seconds. As you do this several times for several seconds each, your Adam's apple will gradually move higher, and you will erase some of the wrinkles in your neck to boot.

According to Dr. Nishiyama, everyone's Adam's apple starts to sag once they reach sixty, and this sagging is particularly noticeable in men. As an aside, in Japanese we call the Adam's apple the "throat buddha," supposedly because the second cervical vertebra and its connecting parts, which were mistakenly thought to be the Adam's apple after cremation, look like a buddha in a sitting position. Even in a still-living body, however, this element of the larynx does a good job of showing us from the outside the important and delicate operations of the throat.

Dr. Nishiyama's book also explains in detail the value of intentional swallowing and karaoke, even suggesting some beneficial karaoke songs (he says that alternating between high and low notes is beneficial, something I am currently trying to figure out how to do when reciting sutras). He contends that if we can prevent aspiration pneumonia, the average

Japanese lifespan could be increased by ten years. If this sounds like something you might be interested in, I hope you will read his book and put his ideas into practice.

The importance of breath is common sense in both the East and the West. The Buddha taught the importance of breathing in his *Ānāpānasati* (Mindfulness of Breath) sutra, and Genesis 2:7 states, "the Lord God formed the man from the dust of the ground and breathed into his nostrils the breath of life, and the man became a living being." But breathing, swallowing, and vocalization are all tasks that the throat alone must perform with exquisite precision, neither too fast nor too slow. No wonder people consider it somehow related to God or the Buddha.

I have heard that when a cat falls from a high place, it will first orient its throat toward the ground, then twist its head and the rest of its body to match. I doubt exercising the laryngeal muscles will allow me to purr like a cat, but if it will raise my Adam's apple and prevent pneumonia, that is good enough for me.

49

Graves and Meadows

I often recall the beautiful grasslands I saw in the highlands of Aso, in Kumamoto Prefecture. Open fields of this sort can be roughly divided into natural and semi-natural meadows, and those in Aso are of the latter type: if left untouched they would eventually become forests, but human activities such as regular cutting, grazing, and controlled burns have instead maintained them as meadows.

The precincts of shrines and temples are another place where repeated human activity such as weeding has kept the ground cleared. Service groups aplenty come to places like the Imperial Palace and Ise Shrine to weed the grounds. Weed-free areas are an expression of Japanese industriousness and aesthetics, and are preserved throughout the country as a part of Japan's beauty. For five centuries, people have been crawling across the grounds of our temple to do the same.

In the past the ground was able to absorb excess water, because stone walls used to be built with gaps in them and there were no paved areas or concrete-lined ditches. Now, however, surroundings are sealed off and weeds are always being pulled, which compacts the soil and makes it impossible for air and water to circulate. Tree roots grow poorly in the resulting hardened soil, and with nothing to hold the topsoil in place, heavy rains easily wash it away. This creates a vicious cycle.

In the last few years, I have started seeing many dead lower branches on our temple's cherry trees. Dead lower branches indicate a problem with surface soil, while dead upper branches indicate problems deeper down. Unwilling to let this progress any further, this year I decided to let the weeds grow wild on our temple's grounds. I even put up a sign explaining the situation: "We are allowing weeds to grow so they will loosen up our temple's soil. Please forgive the unsightliness, and do not pull them."

Hoping to eventually increase the amount of moss growing in our grounds, I collected some juniper moss from a grove of bamboo and transplanted it in places. Rain helps to disperse the moss's spores, increasing the amount that will grow, so this year I have been looking forward to rainy days. I had heard that plants in the grass family with fibrous roots are best for improving soil quality, so I also planted some oats. Unfortunately, I was too lazy to cover more than a portion of them with soil, so flocks of sparrows swooped in and ate most of the seed. In

If you repeatedly cut weeds to the height of their natural bending in the wind, they won't grow so high

Wow!

Revolutionary!

the end, laziness undoes all of one's efforts.

After all this dithering, it is now nearly Obon, and I have started to worry about family graves. Our graveyard is quite large, so if we are going to improve air and water permeability across the entire mountain, we cannot just ignore it.

Under the guidance of Yano Tomonori of the consulting company Mori-no-Engei, who I have mentioned before, I tried "high-cut weeding" along many of the embankments and roads around our graveyard and other areas. My wife called families who had requested year-round maintenance of their graves to ask for their permission, but as it turned out we also ended up cutting the weeds on surrounding gravesites. Specifically, we used sickles and trimmers to cut back growth to the height at which these plants would naturally bend under strong winds, carefully spreading the cut weeds in place. According to Mr. Yano, after repeated cutting to this height weed growth will greatly slow, eventually creating a beautiful meadow-like state. This will also deepen the shadows cast by grasses, making it easier for moss to grow.

I have no doubt, however, that for many of our parishioner families a change of this scale is on par with the Copernican revolution. Some of those who come to thoroughly weed gravesites every year just before Obon did an excellent job as usual, no doubt wondering how things could have gotten as bad as they were. By contrast, many others have gotten fed up with the whole weeding thing and are considering lining their entire gravesite in stone. I hope we can reach the promised "meadow-like state" before such modifications make our soil even less water-permeable.

All we are aiming for is some graves that appear to be sitting in a meadow, although that might be harder to achieve than the sprawling semi-natural grasslands in Aso. I will do my best to convince others over the long term of the advantages of doing so.

50

A Demonstration of Dedication

November 2017

On a recent fine autumn afternoon, I was anticipating the arrival of Kurosawa Yūta, an instructor in swordsmanship at Nihon Butokuin. I knew him casually from Zen meditation sessions, but that day was different. He had told me he wanted to give a demonstration and lecture on swordsmanship, which he had practiced for many years.

Such demonstrations of martial arts were not something I was highly familiar with. For what it's worth, I started practicing kendo at the local dojo in the third grade and belonged to the kendo club in junior and senior high school. To advance levels in kendo, you must use a wooden sword while performing a kata, a routine comprising a fixed pattern of moves. Those, however, were nothing like the sword maneuvers performed by Kurosawa (who in 2018 adopted the sword-master name Ryū'un). He demonstrated the kind of techniques that are only possible with real swords, and they were so different from those in kendo, which developed purely as a sport, that I was stunned. Each of the three swords he removed from black leather cases gleamed ominously. They had a certain presence that made me hyper-aware of them while we sat talking in the main hall.

Since the weather was good, we decided to hold the demonstration in front of our Kannon Hall, which enshrines an Eleven-Headed Kannon image. The living quarters were still being renovated, so many craftspeople were present on the temple grounds. Wanting to give them the chance to see Kurosawa's performance, I sent word that they should gather in front of the Kannon Hall at three thirty.

Normally, Kurosawa's students assist him, but today he had to make do with a few young carpenters and monks. They carried from Kurosawa's car more than a dozen bundles of tatami mats that had been soaked in water overnight, and managed to mount them on stands in time for the performance. In addition to a husband and wife who happened to be paying their respects at a gravesite, over twenty people gathered in front of the hall, including carpenters, foundation layers, pump installers, and electricians. Everyone was watching Kurosawa in his black hakama, wondering what they were about to see.

Without his usual assistants, it probably took him longer than usual to set up between individual demonstrations, causing the show to progress quite slowly. I also suspect the unevenness of the grassy ground made his footing less sure than normal. Once his demonstration began, however, the atmosphere in front of our hall, bathed in the waning afternoon sun, was indescribable. Part of it was likely the aura that Kurosawa emanated as he became one with his sword. Time and space distorted curiously, and I lost track of how long we watched him.

Kendo practitioners use their wooden swords very differently than those who use real swords. Striking with a kendo sword is an instantaneous act that is the full focus of concentration, as indicated by the *kiai* shout that accompanies it. This shout can also be a threatening precursor to attack. An attack is thus followed by a brief release, a momentary lowering of the guard.

In contrast, Kurosawa's swordplay was more fluid. It is no easy task to cut through a human torso, as the sword-wielder is presumably

Kurosawa Yūta,
Sword Instructor, Nihon Butokuin

Slicing through rolls of
soaked tatami mats

Hyaaah!

a. Thick roll: 5 tatami
b. Single roll: 1 tatami

imagining. It requires a more sustained focusing of concentration. He begins to move once his concentration has reached a sufficient level, allowing him to maintain it as he slices through the wet bundles once, and then again. From within this same depth of concentration comes his *kiai*, which seems to exemplify the relaxed alertness that is the goal of martial arts. Kurosawa described this mental state as a way of paying respect to the dead, which did a lot to explain the sadness I sensed in his voice.

Kurosawa concluded his demonstration with a deep bow to our Eleven-Headed Kannon. After watching him drive away in his blue sports car, I spent some time thinking about bushido. Those who wield real swords must constantly take measures to ensure they do not hurt someone. This is the spirit of the *bushi* warrior that *The Chrysanthemum and the Sword* author Ruth Benedict was unable to understand. If you would like to learn more about this, I recommend Kurosawa's book *Shinken* (Sword; Kobunsha, 2008).

51

Unkei and Muda Tomohiro

January 2018

I took a short trip recently, driving first to Tokyo and then to the Izu Peninsula. This was the first time I had driven beyond our neighboring prefectures in quite some time.

I was attending—and uncharacteristically giving a talk at—an exhibition of photographs by Muda Tomohiro at an Izu gallery called Chihan'an, originally built as a private residence around two hundred years ago. There was also an exhibit of works by the Buddhist sculptor Unkei (d. 1223) at the Tokyo National Museum in Ueno, the catalog for which was mainly photographed by Muda. I very much wanted to see it before meeting him in person. That is why I braved the crowded exhibition and went to Izu by way of Ueno.

I stood transfixed in front of Unkei's depictions of Asanga (Jp. Mujaku) and his half-brother Vasubandhu (Jp. Seshin; fl. fourth or fifth century), the primary founders of the Yogācāra school of Buddhism. All the sculptures demonstrated Unkei's unparalleled skill and amazing impressionistic ability, but the images of Asanga and Vasubandhu in particular had a certain air about them that completely enveloped me. Along with the sculptures of deer and a dog said to have been created by his son Tankei (1173–1256), those images remained in my mind as I made my way to Izu.

I arrived at Chihan'an in the town of Izu-Ōhito after nine at night. Muda came out to greet me because the proprietress, Awaya Nobuko, had gone to the local kindergarten to borrow chairs for the following day's event. Muda warmed up the anglerfish stew Ms. Awaya had prepared for us, and we started eating without her as she had requested. She joined us later, and our feast and conversation lasted until after two in the morning.

I had known Muda since we met at another exhibit of his the year before. His photographs are quite exciting. He told me that when presented with a subject, he tries to empty himself and wait, to reflect upon what he will be photographing. He calls this "lowering his consciousness level," but to me it sounds a lot like Zen meditation.

When we see or hear a thing, we instantly position it within a complex map we have created within our brains. By the time we have realized what we are perceiving, countless thoughts have already become involved, including our personal likes, dislikes, and value judgments. The Yogācāra school of Buddhism created by Asanga and Vasubandhu considers the unconscious to be divided into two levels: a shallow self-centered unconscious (*manas-vijñāna*) and a deep unconscious common to all humankind (*ālaya-vijñāna*). I believe that when Muda "lowers

Mr. Muda

Vasubandhu

Asanga

163

his consciousness level," he is considering his subject in a way that goes beyond the shallow *manas-vijñāna* and into the deeper *ālaya-vijñāna*. I also believe that is why his photographs show me things I have never seen before.

The photographs in the Chihan'an exhibit depicted objects he had found while walking through disaster areas after the Tōhoku earthquake and tsunami, removed from the context in which they had been discovered and placed alone on the blank page of a sketchbook. When seen in isolation, they for some reason appear beautiful, which forces us to take pause. Two shallow sets of values—one associated with the context they were photographed in, the other with the context they are exhibited in—start to compete. After a time, I became overly conscious of the place where I was, this two-hundred-year-old room in an art gallery. I was viewing photographs whose context had been removed, but they were now in this new location, giving them a new context. Perhaps that was part of the theme of the exhibition. I felt something similar with the sculptures by Unkei that had been removed from their temple halls.

Muda told me that when he was photographing the statues of Asanga and Vasubandhu, a friend from college had called and told him his leg had been amputated. Because he was in this lower state of consciousness, he hardly reacted to his friend's news. He told me it is particularly easy to lower his consciousness level when photographing Buddhist statues, and that was especially true in this case.

Later, he showed me a book containing his photos of Asanga and Vasubandhu, completely removed from any kind of context. It is interesting, I thought, how a photography book will be viewed in any setting.

52

Hearts

February 2018

I was surprised when I first heard that there are Star of David designs at the Ise Shrine, but this was before the Internet; today all you need to do is type "Star of David" and "Ise Shrine" into a search engine, and you will get thousands of hits. Some of those hits claim this proves the Japanese and the Jews share a common ancestor. But even before reading any of those pages in detail, I recall my own reaction when I first heard about this.

In short, both the Star of David and the iconography at the Ise Shrine are likely intended to represent light, and some agreement between simple forms can be expected, even between East and West. In other words, I felt like simple coincidence might explain the similarity. In fact, in early statues of the seated Bhaiṣajyaguru (Jp. Yakushi), the Medicine Buddha, you can connect the main points to create a star shape.

The same could be said about the shape that is generally called a "heart." I have heard claims that this shape originated in ancient Egypt, or in Greece, but whatever the case, it seems to be a representation of the human heart (or, by some accounts, the outline of a woman's breasts or buttocks) that has spread throughout the world as a symbol of love. The heart symbol used on playing cards first appeared in Germany.

The exact same shape has also been used since ancient times in Japan, where we call it *inome*, or "boar's eye." I started thinking about this when I noticed that this *inome* design is used in the new gable pendants at my temple, Fukujūji. To me, they simply look like hearts, so I could not help but wonder how this design came to be named "boar's eye." Kagami Masayuki, the builder in charge of the entranceway, gave me a good explanation.

Apparently, the design originated in China and arrived in Japan along with Buddhism in the Asuka (538–710) and Nara (710–794) periods. It has been used in Japan ever since, in the decoration of shrines, temples, and various other places; off the top of my head, I can recall seeing the design on gables, *keman* temple decorations, sword guards, and the slits in bells. It is common not only on Buddhist ritual objects, but even places like the fittings on general-use wardrobes.

Kagami claimed the shape is thought to ward off fire and evil spirits, and my own research suggests that this belief originates in *wǔxíng*, the Five Phases of Chinese philosophy. Of the animals in the Chinese zodiac, *wǔxíng* says the boar and rat have "water" characteristics, and since water conquers fire, the boar was selected as a guardian against fire. Of course, you might think if that is the case, then "rat's eye" should work just as well, but there is something about rats that seems less than sacred, and many people have a natural aversion to them, so maybe that is why boars won out. Come to think of it, the *taru-no-kuchi* decoration that juts out from the upper part of Japanese gable pendants is a design based on saké barrel lids, and this motif, too, seemingly has some relation to fire prevention.

At Buddhist temples, we recite sutras for the prevention of fires every morning, which shows just how great a threat fire has been throughout Japan's history. Our temple is also required to perform periodic fire prevention training drills, and we have a prioritized list of what to save

Sacred fig tree leaves ♥

Bells ♥

Sword guards ♥

in the event of a fire.

All of this convinced me of the meaning of the boar's eye design, but I suppose one question remains: does a boar's eye really look like a heart? It is also possible that before any association with boars, this heart-like shape arrived in Chang'an, the predominant international city of the Tang dynasty, via China's Western Regions. I have heard that the *inome* shape is particularly popular in Buddhist circles because of its similarity to the leaf of the sacred fig tree under which the Buddha attained enlightenment. If that is the case, that would explain the popularity of this beautiful shape better than some meaning assigned after the fact. In any event, whether you call it a heart or an *inome*, it is a graceful form that will doubtless remain with us in the future.

53

A Nation's Lands

March 2018

I have been thinking about land lately. Recently, more and more foreigners have been purchasing land in Japan, especially in Hokkaido. But I wonder—can land owned by someone who does not live in that country truly be considered part of that nation? Are there any regulations concerning "national land"?

In ancient times, Japanese people believed that gods inhabited the land itself and that living in a certain place meant being protected by its resident god or gods. Worshipping the gods of the land on which they lived, therefore, would have been their natural duty. Once people started going on about "freedom of religion," however, such beliefs became the prerogative of individuals. There are few enough Japanese with such beliefs these days, so we certainly cannot expect them of foreigners.

I turned to the Japanese constitution, thinking that surely it would have something to say about the handling of the physical land that makes up our nation . . . but there was nothing. Japan's constitution has not a single word to say about land in Japan.

Investigating this further, I found a draft constitution proposed before the adoption of our current constitution that suggested all land should be the property of the state. However, this proposal was aimed at the establishment of a republic following the ideas of Stalin, such as nationalization of land and state control of the means of production.

Acceptance of the Potsdam Declaration forced Japan to reduce the extent of its territory. However, some people took the position that there was no need to revise Japan's constitution (the Constitution of the Empire of Japan) to make stipulations regarding territory, because the constitution did not have any provisions regarding national lands (territory) in the first place. Maybe at the time, they thought the extent of Japan's territory might increase again so they did not want to make any such stipulations during revision.

In today's Japan, many rules related to land use exist despite this lack of fundamental provisions. Take, for example, the Act on Special Measures Concerning Public Use of Deep Underground. Some of my readers might have been surprised to hear about the completion of a road built 55 meters below Tokyo, without permission being obtained from those living above it. As if to provide legal justification for that incident, the above-mentioned law states that so far as public use is concerned, anything deeper than 40 meters below ground, or deeper than 10 meters below the top of supporting bedrock, is fair game. Moreover, this law applies not to the whole country, but only to the three major metropolitan areas of Tokyo, Osaka, and Nagoya; other regions apparently are not considered important enough when it comes to underground development to be worthy of consideration.

If you are going to dig a well, for example, you can dig as deep as you like in most of the islands of Honshu, Kyushu, and Shikoku, but if you are in one of the areas mentioned above, you can only dig to 40 meters. Considering the geography of water veins, shouldn't there be a bit more consistency in how we address such issues?

I also heard that Japan Railways raised 50 billion yen for the reconstruction of Tokyo Station by selling "airspace rights" over the station.

Laws regulating building height vary by location, but so long as your building is within that limit, you can sell rights to the space above it. The purchaser is then able to build on top of your building to whatever height they like, even if that exceeds the supposed limit for that area. It is a completely ridiculous situation, another example of how you can get pretty much anything you want if you have enough money.

For reasons such as this, I am in favor of amending the constitution to include some mention of land use, but by saying so I run the risk of being called a revisionist by constitutional conservatives. I believe there is plenty of room for improving our constitution in ways that have nothing to do with Article 9, which forbids engaging in war or maintaining an offensive army, but both sides need to discuss such issues more calmly, and in more specific terms.

Public use of deep underground

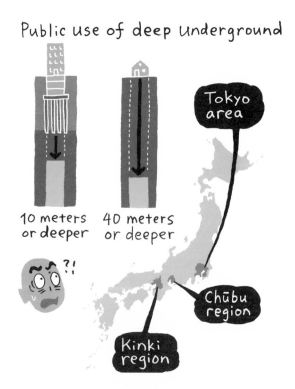

10 meters or deeper

40 meters or deeper

Tokyo area

Chūbu region

Kinki region

54

Sontaku and *Dangō*

April 2018

In the region where I live, it is customary to eat *dango* dumplings at memorial services and other events involving visits to gravesites. These days we sometimes have more modern snacks too, but when the *dango* come out someone will inevitably turn to a child and say: "If you eat this *dango*, you'll become smarter!"

When I hear that, I get annoyed, and I will mutter something about how eating *dango* does not actually make you smarter. Then I will tell anyone who will listen about the wordplay between *dango* dumplings and *dangō*, which means "discussions."

The belief about dumplings making you smart started with the idea that if you take advantage of a group of relatives getting together (such as at a family memorial service), then having a thorough *dangō* (discussion) about what everyone should be doing will prevent future problems, or "headaches." This morphed into eating *dango* to prevent headaches, and that in turn became *dango* making your head work better, in other words, becoming smarter. That last bit feels like one jump too far, however, so when I hear this nonsense about graveside *dango* making you smarter, I take on the unpleasant role of disenchanter-in-chief.

As another example of how the meanings of words can change, the word *dangō* has gone from having a very positive association to a very negative one in Japanese. In Japan's Warring States period (fifteenth–sixteenth centuries), the discussions called *dangō* were a vital element of any victory. After all, when human lives are at stake, who would not want to thoroughly discuss what plans should be made? Today, however, this word has become sullied by the construction industry in particular, where it most commonly refers to "discussions" that result in bid rigging. This has now become part of the dictionary definition of the word, and is the sense in which the vast majority of the public understands it. I have even heard a child joking that "if you're smart enough to *dangō*, you probably don't need *dango*," at which point I just had to laugh and give up any hope for this word regaining its original meaning.

Another wonderful word that is in serious decline is *sontaku*, which means to gauge how someone else feels. The Chinese philosopher Mencius (372–289 BCE) considered our capacity for compassion to be the basis of inherent human goodness, so an ability to read others' emotions would be quite welcome. For his part, Confucius (c. 551–479 BCE) taught a version of the Golden Rule: "What you do not wish for yourself, do not do to others." Putting this ideal into practice does indeed require *sontaku*—that is, the ability to ask yourself whether those around you desire one thing or another. *Sontaku* will always be at work where there is compassion, namely the ability to feel pity for the misfortune of others.

Mencius, by the way, believed humans have four characteristic emotions: compassion, disdain, respect, and approval. Of these, compassion is particularly important, being the basis for righteousness (from which arises disdain), propriety (from which arises respect), and wisdom (from which arises approval). I believe *sontaku* will continue to be an important mental function, thanks to its role in supporting compassion.

Until recently, *sontaku* was a somewhat archaic term, but unfortunately, it has returned to general use in connection with an ongoing political scandal in Japan: the serious crime of altering official documents, supposedly to conform with the presumed wishes of superiors. While that association may not be enough to discredit the inherent goodness of humans, use of the word will almost certainly be associated with wrongdoing for some time.

Working in a way that will maximally please your boss is a fine idea, and one that might even enhance workplace motivation, but I wonder why some people, before acting on what they presume to be the boss's wishes, cannot just pause and straightforwardly ask whether what they are doing really is desired. Wouldn't that be better than acting under misguided *sontaku*? After all, acting without knowing whether what you

are doing is truly what is desired is nothing more than self-righteousness.

Imagining an answer without bothering to ask the question cannot be the proper form of *sontaku*. If we are not careful, *sontaku* devolves into prejudice or self-righteousness and compassion becomes unwelcome kindness. Respect becomes forced, and we can no longer distinguish between right and wrong.

I believe the above-mentioned scandal occurred not due to any inherent human "badness," nor because there is something wrong with *sontaku* itself, but because we create situations in which questions cannot be asked. It is that atmosphere in the halls of Japan's government, and what happens when mistaken assumptions backfire, that worries me most.

55

Nurturing Life:
Crows and Crouching *Dogū* Figurines

May 2018

Seeing a crow flying in the evening sky, I was reminded of a Japanese children's song:

> *Mother crow, mother crow, to whom do you call so?*
> *I call to my seven lovely children, who live up on the mountain.*
> *Oh how lovely, oh how lovely, I cry.*
> *You're so lovely, oh so lovely, I cry.*
> *Go to the mountains and see the old nest I have there.*
> *You will see the sweet, round-eyed children I have there.*

This in turn reminded me of something I heard in college from a study-abroad student from China. She had learned this song in her Japanese class, she said, but she just could not understand how a baby crow could be "lovely." How curious, she thought: whether child or mother, a crow is just a crow.

I am sure she is not the only one who feels that way. Indeed, there are probably few people in the world who genuinely like those jet-black birds. Despite crows in the US and Europe being slightly smaller than they are in Japan, they are equally disliked there, and in Hawaii, people actually brag about how no crows live there—the islands are too far from the continent for crows to fly there, and thankfully none have managed to stow away on ships. Adult crows are very much despised in Japan, possibly because of their black feathers, or possibly because their intelligence is viewed as cunning.

I have often wondered what the world would think of crows if they were white. As smart as they are, if they were a pure, snowy white, wouldn't people praise them every time they saw them? And if they were praised on a daily basis, wouldn't that greatly change their personality? As a dazzling white bird of wisdom and good fortune, crows might even be seen as contributing to human society. This is the conclusion I always arrive at. But there is no point in speculating about such impossible scenarios. Rather, it is more important to consider how we might look at crows and see "good, round-eyed children," and imagine a mother crow crying "oh, so lovely."

After some thought, I have concluded that this does not just apply to mother crows. A poem by the Buddhist priest Gyōki (668–749) goes:

> In the cooing of the pheasant
> I hear the call of my father, of my mother,

and a haiku by Bashō (1644–1694) says:

> When I hear pheasants
> I mourn the passing of my
> Father and mother.

It is interesting how these two well-known poets both saw love between parents and children in the cries of birds.

Many *dogū* clay figurines were created during Japan's Jōmon period (c. 14,000–300 BCE). Much mystery still surrounds these objects, but some were clearly made to reflect themes of pregnancy, childbirth, and child-rearing. Particularly interesting is the "crouching *dogū*" that was excavated from the Kamioka ruins in my home prefecture of Fukushima. It may represent a woman giving birth in a squatting position, which was common in Japan until the Edo period (1603–1867), or possibly a woman comforting a crying child, but whatever the case, one can feel encapsulated within its form ancient people's prayers and feelings of sanctitude with regards to pregnancy and childbirth. This figure was designated as an important cultural property of Japan in 2011, and is currently on display at the Jomopia Miyahata archaeological park in Fukushima.

Not to complain about Mother's Day and carnations, which arrived in Japan in the twentieth century, but perhaps it would be worthwhile to pay less attention to how other countries celebrate motherhood and instead turn our attention now and then to the gods worshipped by the ancient people of our own country, as represented by the "crouching *dogū*." Nurturing another life within oneself through pregnancy and childbirth is, after all, a model of the compassion we pursue in Buddhism.

Crouching clay figurine

Fukushima City

An object of fertility worship?

But the positioning of the arms is puzzling...

56

Cuckoos and Warblers

July 2018

I can hear lesser cuckoos in the mountain behind our temple, and warblers in our gardens. Japanese bush warblers begin their youthful, innocent songs with the arrival of spring, when plum trees blossom, but have now moved on to a far more complex call. Sometimes I wonder if they are not singing just to revel in the sound of their own voices. In contrast, here in northeastern Japan, cuckoos start singing in the deep green mountains around the end of May. I understand that they spend the winter in a region that stretches from India to southern China, returning to Japan once the caterpillars they love to eat start to emerge.

I have heard that birds with Japanese names ending in -me or -su are named after the sounds of their calls, which is the part coming before that suffix. Examples include swallows (*tsubame*), sparrows (*suzume*), crows (*karasu*), and jays (*kakesu*). How very Japanese, I thought, to simply call birds by the sounds they make.

Following that rule, however, a Japanese bush warbler (*uguisu*) would sound like "*ugui*" and a lesser cuckoo (*hototogisu*) would sound like "*hototogi*," which is a bit of a stretch. Cuckoos in particular tell different tales depending on who is listening in which part of Japan. I have heard their call described as sounding like *honzon-kaketa-ka* ("hang

the temple's main icon painting") and *teppen-kaketa-ka* ("run to the top")
and *tokkyo-kyoka-kyoku* ("patent permissions office"), but in my region,
we say they sound like *potto-ottsaketa* ("Look, he's split his belly"). That
is what I was told when I was growing up, at least, so that is what it
sounds like when I hear them.

It is rare to actually spot a lesser cuckoo or a bush warbler, so their
calls are what I most associate with them. This is especially true for the
cuckoos, who tend to be active at times when humans are not, at night-
time and around dawn, making their calls particularly enticing.

Lesser cuckoos are also called *fujoki* in Japanese, a name that comes
from Chinese mythology. In the old Chinese kingdom of Shu, there was
a man named Duyu who later became Emperor Wang Di. He retired to
the mountains where he later died, but after his death, he transformed

into a cuckoo, flying about and using his shrill call to inform the people when it was time to start farming each year. When Shu later fell to Qin Shi Huang (259–210 BCE), the First Emperor of Qin, the transformed Duyu is said to have cried "you'd best return, you'd best return!" (the Japanese reading of which is *fujoki*) until it spit blood, and that is why the inside of a cuckoo's mouth is red.

Poet Masaoka Noboru's (1867–1902) pen name Shiki is another word for "cuckoo," which he likely adopted for this "cry until you spit blood" imagery. Or perhaps he would have said he chose it because of the bird's striking appearance: black and gray overall, but with yellow rings around its eyes and a reddish beak.

Interestingly, if you listen to the lesser cuckoo's call without any preconceived notions, all you hear is chirping birdsong, which is enough to transport you deep into the mountains. One of my favorite haiku (as a big fan of bonito tuna), by Yamaguchi Sodō (1642–1716), describes some of the things he associates with early summer:

> Green leaves everywhere,
> the call of lesser cuckoos,
> taste of bonito.

There is a reason why lesser cuckoos and Japanese bush warblers start singing in the mountains at around the same time. All this singing is, of course, in the name of finding a mate, so the indirect result of birdsong is bird eggs. It is important for the cuckoos to produce their eggs at the same time as the warblers because, as you may know, cuckoos lay their eggs in the nests of other birds. While it may seem crafty for cuckoos to relegate egg hatching and child-rearing duties to warblers and other birds, research has shown that they do not have an impressive success rate. Other birds will of course chase them off if they are discovered while trying to invade a nest, and their parasitic eggs are sometimes noticed and tossed out.

When I thought about these dark events unfolding in the mountain behind our temple, I recalled the "baby box" that was recently set up in Kumamoto as a way for women to abandon newborns they could not care for, and the many Buddhist monks in olden times who came from poor families. It seems that from ages past, systems have existed for supporting the abandoned young of not just birds and beasts, but humans as well.

Just now, again, I heard the piercing cry of a cuckoo, signaling the imminent arrival of summer.

57

Cleaning the Pond

August 2018

I would like to tell you about something we did the other day for the first time in a long while: cleaning the pond that has been a part of our temple grounds for I don't know how many centuries.

Over many years, a layer of silt and organic matter collects at the bottom and must occasionally be cleaned. I looked forward to this when I was a child because it was a chance to catch pond snails and crucian carp. Young people these days are strangers to such delicacies, but they used to be quite a treat. We would put the snails in miso soup or simmer them with vegetables, and the carp would usually be boiled and sweetened. Back then, many people would climb into the pond and use nets and the like to chase the fish. This would stir up all the silt, making it not very efficient, but I suppose that inefficiency was part of the fun.

Pond-cleaning today is quite a different affair. The company I hired brought a pump, but before using it, one of the workers sprinkled the water with an interesting substance called Neonite. He said it was a "water purification agent." As soon as he added the whitish powder, the water started to clear up, with largish chunks of what looked like mud collecting and sinking to the bottom. Neonite reportedly has no effect on living things, so its use is becoming widespread throughout Japan.

The product is manufactured in Shimane Prefecture, where it is used to purify water that will be released into Lake Shinji; that lake is famous for its clams, so dirty water is not allowed to flow into it. Similar strict regulations on water flowing into the Seto Inland Sea have made this product popular in western Japan, but it has also been used to decontaminate reservoirs following the Tōhoku earthquake. The product causes suspended solids to clump, which makes pumping easier and increases the options for disposal.

The worker presiding over our pond cleanup poured the Neonite into the water, gave it a good stir, and let it sit overnight. It was fun to watch the water clear, gradually revealing fish I had never seen before. Mostly they were just crucian carp, koi, and goldfish, but still, I could see movement in a pond that had previously been too muddy to see anything.

The pond is also home to many bullfrogs, but I did not see any even after the water level had become quite low. I did not hear them, either. They are large but quite agile, and just as I was wondering if they had evacuated and were hiding somewhere, I saw a suspicious shadow dart beneath a rhododendron bush.

I imagine that from their perspective, we were intruders in their home and garden, and they likely considered themselves to be in great danger. As one nimbly jumped away from the now nearly dry pond, I heard a high-pitched cry very unlike the ordinary croak of a bullfrog. I had been wondering if our pond cleaner might not also take the frogs away for us. But seeing this made me realize how futile the effort would be.

The worker dragged a vacuum hose through the pond, and after that, used a tool like a squeegee to dredge its bottom. He told me that he is forty-two now and has only recently gotten into the water business, having previously worked in the mountains on flood-control construction projects. He wore a full-body wetsuit and remained in the pond the entire time, while the company president strode about in galoshes between the pond and the place where they were dumping sludge, telling jokes and conversing with the four employees who were there as he went.

I had a good time myself, walking the path to the pond and back many times yesterday and today. I felt as if that company president had shown me how the head of an organization should act. Maybe that explains why this company based in the city of Iwaki gets called to various parts of Fukushima Prefecture. Thanks to them, I spent a refreshing time before the end of the rainy season.

58

The Virtue of Shadows

September 2018

I cannot see the word "shadows" without thinking of Tanizaki Jun'ichirō's (1886–1965) *In Praise of Shadows*. Written in 1933 and published in two parts, it presents a theory of civilization that remains very interesting even when read today, or perhaps particularly when read today. Tanizaki, one of Japan's most famous novelists, provides deep and insightful commentary on a wide variety of topics, including architecture, gardens, tableware, meals, kabuki, noh, and makeup, but his core message is a warning that because Japanese culture is cultivated in the shadows, we should not rashly turn up the lights. Indeed, the Japanese word for "rashly" is written using kanji meaning "without darkness," which should tell us something. "Without darkness," to the Japanese, means thoughtlessness and recklessness, a lack of room for deliberation and contemplation.

I understand that lacquerware was once so closely associated with Japan that it was called "japan" in English. Tanizaki describes lacquerware as being most beautiful when viewed by lamplight or candlelight. Here is his assessment:

There are good reasons why lacquer soup bowls are still

used, qualities which ceramic bowls simply do not possess. . . . With lacquerware there is a beauty in that moment between removing the lid and lifting the bowl to the mouth when one gazes at the still, silent liquid in the dark depths of the bowl, its color hardly differing from that of the bowl itself. What lies within the darkness one cannot distinguish, but the palm senses the gentle movements of the liquid, vapor rises from within forming droplets on the rim, and the fragrance carried upon the vapor brings a delicate anticipation. What a world of difference there is between this moment and the moment when soup is served Western style, in a pale, shallow bowl. A moment of mystery, it might almost be called, a moment of trance.*

If this short passage has left you wanting more, I urge you to read the entire book, but here I would first like to introduce one more example of the virtue of shadows that Tanizaki points out.

In the latter half of *In Praise of Shadows*, Tanizaki describes someone returning to Japan from Paris a few years before the essay was published and commenting that Tokyo and Osaka are far more brightly lit at night than any European city. "Perhaps no two countries in the world waste more electricity than America and Japan, he said, for Japan is only too anxious to imitate America in every way it can."** He then describes the president of the Kaizōsha publishing house taking Albert Einstein (1879–1955) to Kyoto.

Looking out the train window, Einstein points to "an electric lamp burning in broad daylight," regarding which he states, "Now that is terribly wasteful."

Apparently, then, a growing insensitivity toward shadows in Japan is nothing new. Tanizaki sums it up as follows: "So benumbed are we nowadays by electric lights that we have become utterly insensitive to the evils of excessive illumination."*** Tanizaki specifically mentions the excessive use of lighting in teahouses, restaurants, inns, and hotels, in which no unlit corner remains. Not only does this tarnish Japanese aesthetics, it produces a lot of heat. Places intended for cooling off on summer evenings are lit up before dusk, making them less cool. *In Praise of Shadows* closes with Tanizaki's suggestion that we try turning off our lights, however difficult that may be.

Looking back, the two brightest places I have ever been were a pachinko parlor and the dormitory for a three-day, two-night course on a new religion. On the final day, after having endured a sleepless night, I was forced to recite something under glaring lights. It was an experience that stripped away my capacity for rational thought and diluted any emotion I might have experienced. To me, it felt like a form of brainwashing.

---

* Tanizaki Jun'ichirō, *In Praise of Shadows*, trans. Thomas Harper and Edward Seidensticker (Leete's Island Books, 1977), 15.

** Ibid., 35.

*** Ibid., 36.

59

The Attractiveness of Walls and *Tataki* Floors

October 2018

Some architectural terms in Japanese are native words, while others are loanwords from other languages. Our words for "exterior walls," "fence," and "gate," for example, come from Chinese. This suggests to me that the Japanese had somewhat less interest in separating the inside from the outside than did the Chinese. Come to think of it, while stone walls became predominant in Japan's Warring States period (fifteenth–sixteenth centuries), hedges were more common before that. So, apparently, people felt less of a need for highly secure protection back then.

Our word for interior walls (*kabe*), however, is native Japanese. The word originally referred not only to divisions between rooms but also to structural materials. Being a Japanese word, we can assume that it developed along with the country. Walls in Japan were originally made from materials such as earth, plaster, boards, and stone, but bricks were added to that list in the Meiji era, and concrete and drywall after World War II.

Reflecting on postwar architecture, I cannot help but feel we have deviated from the building techniques and materials that are best suited to Japan, in particular, to our high humidity and frequent earthquakes.

We are nearing completion of construction on the living quarters at our temple, and the plasterers have started working on the walls. In discussions with Maeda Shinji, chief architect at Kurashijusshoku Architects Office, we decided to make all the walls out of either plaster, diatomaceous earth, or *juraku* clay, depending on the location. In places prone to humidity, we are using diatomaceous earth because it absorbs excess moisture, and we are using *juraku* clay in places where shadows should be emphasized because of its interesting texture. Most of the walls, however, will be plaster. This is because plaster is the most durable of the three materials, is resistant to both fire and earthquakes, and naturally absorbs odors.

All three wall materials do an excellent job of absorbing air and water, so they are well suited to the humid climate of Japan. This is particularly important because of the pond near the building. Regarding earthquake resistance, it is unfortunate that Japanese building standards do not yet permit use of the *ishibadate* method of placing pillars on stones rather than embedding them in the ground, nor can we use the old-style *komaikabe* wattle and daub walls, but we have nevertheless designed wooden structures that we hope will be able to return to their original shape if they are shaken out of place.

I am also looking forward to seeing the new *tataki* floor in the entranceway as much as (or more than) I am looking forward to the walls. *Tataki* is created from earth, lime, and *nigari* (a natural salt solution), so it is written with the kanji 三和土 meaning "three harmonious soils," but because it is pounded into an excellent hardness, those kanji are read as *tataki*, which means "beating." While that name reveals the essence of how this material is created, there are unfortunately few remaining craftspersons who are familiar with the process. Even floors made from concrete are being called *tataki* these days, which is truly sad.

The quality of traditional *tataki* depends on the proportions of sand

and clay present in the soil, so there are no fixed ratios that can be applied to all soils. Since you cannot predict how it will dry until you have made it, some trial-and-error is involved, but there are so few orders for these floors that finding opportunities to gain the necessary experience is difficult.

I have heard that an ideal *tataki* floor allows air and moisture to pass freely through the underground soil and is hard enough that scratching it will not leave marks. The previous living quarters had a *tataki* floor, which not only had a nice color, but also cooled you down during the summertime, while in winter it remained relatively warm. It thus provided an excellent buffer between the inside and outside of the building.

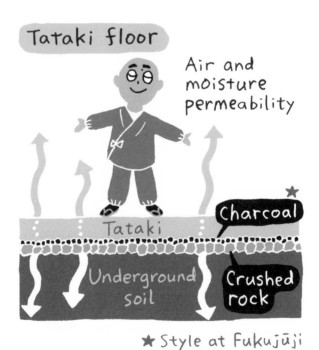

Tataki floor

Air and moisture permeability

Tataki

Charcoal

Underground soil

Crushed rock

★ Style at Fukujūji

But whether it is our walls or *tataki* or shoji sliding doors, I wonder why Japanese homes only weakly isolate spaces? We also go out of our way to make our exterior walls, fences, and gates—Chinese-derived elements, as mentioned above—full of holes and spaces.

I recently heard about a movement to incorporate requirements for airtightness and high-performance insulation into Japan's building standards. It astonishes me that such a thing is happening in Japan, and I can only hope such foolishness will end.

60

Gold and Silver

November 2018

Long ago in Japan, gold and silver were considered to have equal value but different attributes. There was a silver standard for money in western Japan and a gold standard in eastern Japan. There is no common standard that can be applied to both; from the perspective of gold, silver is dim and unexciting, while from silver's perspective, gold is overly shiny and ostentatious. Rather than setting them in competition through comparison, however, the Japanese were able to view both as valuable in their own way. Here again, as discussed earlier in *"The Chrysanthemum and the Sword* and Duality," we see the concept of "duality" derived from the Chinese classic *Zhuangzi*.

This idea permeates various aspects of Japanese culture. For example, the Japanese language uses both Chinese kanji and Japanese kana, and the contrasting spheres of private and public have been recognized since the time of Prince Shōtoku (574–622). Also as discussed before, whenever one facet of Japanese culture comes to the forefront, an opposing force seems to arise as if to restrain the first and prevent it from becoming dominant, as with ostentatiousness in the face of austerity.

We even have conflicting sayings, such as "do good with haste" versus "if you're in a hurry, take the long way," and "lying leads to thievery" versus "lies are expedient." We say "genius appears in childhood" and "great talent blooms late" with approximately the same frequency. In other words, I believe the Japanese have created a culture based on intuition, one that searches for the best approach according to circumstance, rather than always blindly adhering to a single principle. This habit of trying to find the optimal way of living between two extremes is well suited to the "middle way" the Buddha espoused, and also fosters acceptance and kindness toward those who think differently than we do.

Today, of course, silver is widely considered to be worth less than gold, perhaps due to the influence of the Olympics. I also feel that our society has become more insistent on Olympic victories and other symbolic wins that vindicate our drive to constantly go faster, farther, and more efficiently. These values reflect the virtues of Olympians, as well as market principles. In recent years, the Japanese government has prioritized the market principles known as Abenomics over all else, blindly pressing on wherever it leads. The recent scandal in which government agencies were found to be exaggerating the numbers of disabled persons they employ is a natural outcome. National and prefectural institutions like the Ministry of Health, Labour and Welfare, which should be setting an example for the rest of the country, were instead cheating by claiming some seven thousand retirees and people with poor eyesight and the like as "disabled." This is a serious, far-reaching problem, on par with the falsification of official documents as we have seen in another recent scandal.

An investigative committee called the incident an "extremely grave situation" resulting from an "arbitrary interpretation of the scope and method for confirming persons with disabilities," but empty statements such as this do nothing to address the source of the problem—namely the fact that we have become a society that views silver as inferior to gold. We have come to believe the sayings that tell us to "do good with haste," "lies are expedient," and "genius appears in childhood," while paying no attention to "slow" and "honest" and "late blooming." How can we not suffer as a result?

There are many people with disabilities who are incredibly honest, charitable, and kind. Yes, they may be inferior by the measure of market principles, but the problem is precisely that our society has forgotten values other than market principles.

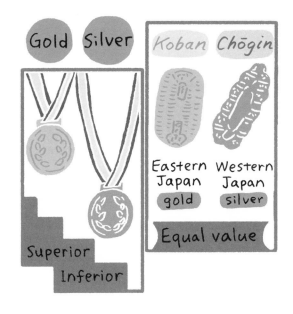

It has recently become easy to diagnose Down syndrome before a baby is born, leading to more prospective parents receiving this diagnosis. Some choose to abort the fetus as a result. I recently heard a mother who had lost a young child with Down syndrome say, "If every home had a child like ours, I don't think there would be any more war. I'm sorry to hear that in the future, fewer people will have the wonderful experience I did."

In Japanese we refer to restrained excellence as "tarnished silver," a stately display of value that need not be showy. If you are used to the values associated with gold, this can be an unexpected discovery of worth. I believe a society that can appreciate the duality of silver and gold is exactly the kindhearted society we should be aiming for.

61

Sayōnara

January 2019

I think there is a great deal of depth to Japanese greetings. Within *konnichiwa* (lit. this day) are expectations for a today that differs from yesterday, suggesting that today is the perfect day for a new start. In Buddhist terms, it describes cessation and reappearance, a termination of the self of yesterday and a rebirth for today. Particularly since the Tōhoku earthquake, I am sure many people have relied on such concepts as a way to recover from their sadness.

Similarly, *konbanwa* (lit. this evening) invites a different feeling from that of the afternoon. The Polish-American diplomat Zbigniew Brzezinski (1928–2017) wrote *The Fragile Blossom: Crisis and Change in Japan* (New York: Harper and Row, 1972) based on his experience living here, and described the Japanese as acting Protestant by day and Mediterranean by night. I suspect he had a lot of fun most nights he was here.

Well then, what about the word we use when parting, *sayōnara*? While I am fond of both *konnichiwa* and *konbanwa* for their uncommon nuance, I believe *sayōnara* to be the most heartbreakingly beautiful of the three. Somewhat ironically, it describes the feeling of not wanting to part, but instead to remain together forever. However, knowing the other person must leave for whatever reason, the speaker expresses understanding as *sayōnara*, which literally means "if it must be so." If true understanding is not possible, the speaker still considers the feelings and circumstances of the other party and acquiesces, stating "Well then, if that's the case, I suppose we must part." *Sayōnara* feels like a word to be spoken in a hushed voice, with feelings held at bay so as not to reveal one's disappointment.

Come to think of it, as a priest charged with officiating at funerals, my job is a series of *sayōnaras*. The other day I sent off a young man who had only just turned twenty-four. His love of the mountains had motivated him to attend Shinshū University near the Japanese Alps, where he joined the mountaineering club and often went climbing. His grandparents had doted on him as their first grandchild, and apparently his love of the mountains first blossomed on fishing trips with his grandfather. After graduation he had become a court clerk as he had hoped, and last November passed the exam for promotion to a senior position. He had returned home over the November holidays to announce the good news. He also took his grandmother to a hot spring, discussed some private matters with his younger sister, and helped his mother with the cooking.

He then returned to the apartment where he lived alone, went for a night drive as was his custom, and while he somehow made it back home, he died of a heart attack right there in his car. The autopsy showed that he had died at around 5:00 a.m., with the same expression on his face as when he had been sleeping at his parents' home just a couple of days before.

At his funeral, over one hundred former classmates and fellow mountaineers sat facing his smiling portrait, though I expect neither they nor his family were able to understand what had happened or view it as something that "must be so." It is the same with natural disasters—

Konnichiwa

Sayōnara

we have no choice but to accept the damage caused by typhoons, earthquakes, and tsunamis, regardless of our feelings about it. We can only move on in the spirit of *konnichiwa*, renewing ourselves with the new day.

I gave this young man a dharma name with characters meaning "verdant mountains" and "light of mercy." The first is from a line of poetry that states "wherever we go, we can find verdant mountains," an expression of the idea that even if we venture beyond our native place, we can find a new place where we would be happy to die. This young man found that place earlier than most, and in the future, we will bathe in the gentle light of his memory.

I do not expect this to help his loved ones embrace the meaning of *sayōnara*. But even so, we must accept the way things are despite not wanting to part. At his funeral I gave a loud *katsu* shout, hoping to help along my own acceptance: "How's winter in the mountains? Are you getting used to the cold? Buckle down and go beyond!"

62

Driving in Robes

On 16 September 2018, the Fukui Prefectural police issued a traffic ticket to a Buddhist priest in his forties for driving in his robes. The claim was that his robes interfered with his driving, but in a later clarification, the police asserted that the problem was not with his robes themselves, but how he was wearing them. Specifically, the priest was wearing a *hakue* white robe that reached to around his ankles, and over that another robe with approximately 30-centimeter sleeves. Because the *hakue* kept his thighs and knees tightly together, the police said, and because his sleeves might get caught on the car's instrumentation, his clothing posed an "obstruction to safe driving."

This caused online pushback from priests nationwide, who flocked to Twitter to post videos of themselves performing various activities under the hashtag #ICanDoItInMyRobes (in Japanese, #僧衣でできるもん). Included among those were priests jumping rope, juggling, skateboarding, playing with *kendama* cup-and-ball toys, and more. Even some secular posters joined in, such as martial artists demonstrating sword-drawing techniques while wearing robes. The overall humorous tone received praise both in Japan and abroad. The point these priests and their supporters were trying to make was, of course, that once you get used to wearing robes you can do pretty much anything in them, and that includes driving.

If you take the reasoning of the prefectural police at face value, the problem was how the priest wore his robes, but in truth, it seems a simple matter of sleeve and hem lengths. If that is the case, the same should apply to most women's kimonos. In fact, the priest's robes in question here had the same hem length as a kimono, but shorter sleeves.

There are of course all kinds of priests' robes. The priest who got the traffic ticket was wearing a *fuhō*, the simplest form of outer-layer robe. I could maybe see an issue if he were wearing one of our more complex, formal robes, but if even a *fuhō* cannot be worn, then pretty much all Buddhist garb is forbidden. This is probably one reason why there was such a loud outcry from other clergy. Some even posted photos of Christian ministers in their vestments. Indeed, if this new restriction becomes the law of the land, I am not sure how I will get to *makura-gyō* (sutra recitations at bedside after death) and funerals. I guess I could change clothes after arriving, but there are certain situations where I do not feel right showing up in everyday priest's garb.

As it turns out, as this essay was being edited, the police announced they were dropping charges against the driving priest. I do not know if they were reacting to the backlash they had received, but in any case, I think the root problem was a misunderstanding of traditional Japanese clothing. I do not know the age of the police officer who issued the ticket, but they must have been young enough to consider Japanese clothing incredibly restrictive.

Typical robes in Rinzai Zen Buddhism have sleeves that are around 73 centimeters long. I must admit they do sometimes get in the way with their flapping about, but we have *tamadasuki* to help with that when driving or performing other tasks. These are cords attached to the inside of both sleeves that allow us to quickly gather them together behind the back. Different sects have different names for and ways of using these cords, but regardless, we monks have had strategies for keeping our sleeves out of the way for centuries.

There are also ways to make sure robes do not interfere with your legs while driving, such as raising them before sitting and tucking the excess cloth beneath your rear. This allows me to drive without any particular inconvenience, but I suppose that is not something a young police officer would necessarily be aware of.

Of course, it would be lovely if this incident became a catalyst for developing robes that improve mobility while retaining the required dignity. Most important, however, is for people to understand that traditional Japanese clothing and priests' robes are far easier to move in than appearances may suggest. I hope everyone can come to understand this in a humorous way by watching priests' antics on Twitter.

Goods for safe driving in kimonos

Stylish sleeve clips and cords

Keep a pair of shoes that don't hinder driving

63

Hansōbō

In early March 2019, I visited the temple Hōkōji in Hamamatsu, Shizuoka Prefecture. I went there to stand witness at a ceremony announcing a newly ordained chief abbot, Yasunaga Sodō, who trained at the same Zen monastery I did. After leaving the Tenryūji monastery, Yasunaga had worked to train the younger generations at international Zen centers and as a professor at Hanazono University. He then received an invitation to become abbot of Hōkōji, the headquarters of the Hōkō sect of Rinzai Buddhism, which he accepted. Thus the ceremony. We were blessed with wonderful weather, and the early cherry blossoms were out, making for a truly lovely day.

A curious figure is enshrined at Hōkōji, the Hansōbō Daigongen. This deity is also enshrined at Kenchōji in Kamakura and Heirinji in Saitama Prefecture, so some of my readers may have encountered him before. His story goes back to Mumon Gensen (1323–1390), the founder of Hōkōji. The son of Emperor Go-Daigo (1288–1339), Mumon entered Ken'ninji in Kyoto the year after his father's death, and in the late Yuan dynasty (1271–1368) traveled to China to study. On his return to Hakata, his ship encountered a storm. Just as the ship's mast threatened to snap in the strong winds and rain, an *ijin* ("strange person" or

Traditional clothing is an important cultural aspect of every cou
and I would like to see more people wearing such clothing. Safe dri
is of course important, but I also hope we can preserve kimono
other traditional garb as a part of Japanese culture.

"foreigner") dressed in priest's robes and with an oddly large nose appeared, took control of the ship, and encouraged the other sailors to hang on as he safely guided them back to Hakata. This mysterious figure was Hansōbō.

When Mumon later founded the Hōkōji at the invitation of Okuyama Rokurōjirō Tomofuji, Hansōbō reappeared, asking to become Mumon's disciple. When Mumon said, "I'm not sure who you are," Hansōbō replied, "I'm half a monk [hansō], everybody says so," and this is how he got his name. He served Mumon by chopping wood, fetching water, and otherwise taking care of him until Mumon died. Hansōbō then said, "I will protect this mountain and this temple, relieve people's suffering, and protect them from disaster," and with that, he vanished.

Afterwards a number of curious events occurred that seemed to suggest Hōkōji was truly being protected. In a forest fire in 1881, only those buildings related to Mumon and Hansōbō were spared, leading to their being enshrined across the country as patrons of maritime safety, fire prevention, and all forms of divine grace.

But just who was this self-styled "half monk" Hansōbō? At Kenchō-ji there are several statues of karasu-tengu, crow-like supernatural beings who were said to be his companions, and some have suggested that Hansōbō was a tengu as well. Others say he was an incarnation of the Shintō deity Sarutahiko.

Tengu are described in various places as tall, white-haired creatures with ruddy complexions and large noses, wearing Buddhist priests' robes. A straightforward interpretation of this suggests that what people called tengu were actually Westerners who had come to study as monks at Zen temples in China at the time, since in thirteenth-century China people were already arriving from the Middle East and Europe to study Buddhism.

Until quite recently, the word ijin was used to describe foreigners, particularly Westerners, as in Noguchi Ujō's 1922 poem "Red Shoes." The word can be considered a contraction of a phrase meaning "person from another country," but that does not convey the heavy connotation of "otherness" that *ijin* has, particularly in terms of appearance. An *ijin*, the word implies, is someone you cannot consider quite human like yourself. Even so, I suspect that during the Muromachi period (1336–1573), Hōkōji was accepting such *ijin* as practitioners.

As son of Emperor Go-Daigo, Mumon must have known that Ashikaga Takauji (1305–1358) had served then later betrayed his father, yet nonetheless later built Tenryūji in dedication to him. He must have also been aware of Musō Soseki's (1275–1351) philosophy of "treating your allies and your enemies alike." Perhaps that philosophy

Zen master
Mumon Gensen   Hansōbō

Yasunaga Sodō

of compassion explains why Hōkōji once provided hospital facilities for leprosy patients.

When Abbot Yasunaga Sodō was in college, he loved rock and roll and often played Eric Clapton songs on his guitar. Since becoming a monk, he has been equally passionate about spiritual exchange between East and West and frequently engages in dialogue with Christians. This makes him the perfect abbot for Hansōbō's Hōkōji. I expect to soon see long lines of Westerners wanting to study under him.

64
A Very Local Move

June 2019

These days, we at Fukujūji Temple are busy with our move. Mentioning that on the telephone one day, the person I was speaking with was quite surprised. "What? You're relocating the temple?" Ah, of course, I thought. When you tell someone you are moving, they will naturally assume you are relocating to some distant place, which is not something they would expect a temple to do. What is actually happening is that we are moving from our temporary rooms in the temple's Monjudō Hall to the newly refurbished living quarters. In other words, we are moving from one building to another within the temple grounds.

When I was a college student living in Tokyo's Minato Ward, I actually experienced a situation in which a temple disappeared overnight. I am sure it was standing there the evening before, solid as anything, because I remember admiring the roof tiles on its main hall as I passed by. The following morning, however, there was just an empty lot studded with foundation stones. Those living in the neighborhood were asking each other what could have possibly happened to it. I heard someone nearby wondering aloud whether a fleet of helicopters came in the night to carry it away, and an elderly woman replying she would have heard them if that was the case.

I hope you will forgive me for bringing up an inexplicable aside and then curtly returning to the main topic, but today I want to talk about the move at our temple, setting aside the mystery of the disappearing temple for another day.

Moving between buildings on the same grounds is harder than it sounds. We hired movers to carry large furniture and such, but that left many smaller articles behind, meaning we had to make many round trips of over one hundred paces each way, carrying clothing and books and sundry other old items. During that time, our telephone was installed, but the intercom was still in the Monjudō Hall. If I was not able to reach the intercom in time to tell visitors to come to the living quarters, I had to walk some eighty steps through the main hall.

The shoe rack in the entranceway to the new living quarters is not finished yet, and the place is currently being used to store the carpenters' tools. This is confusing for visitors trying to figure out where to enter, so today we finally moved our mailbox and newspaper receptacle to where the new intercom is and posted a sign in the Monjudō entranceway telling visitors "Please come to the priest's quarters."

Amidst all this confusion, during one of my countless trips back and forth through the main hall, I heard the doorbell ring. It was a pair of parishioners, a brother and sister who had come from Kanagawa Prefecture to discuss something with me.

I guided them to our new parlor, where no guests had ever sat, and we sat in front of a brazier in which no fire had ever been lit. We started talking there, then walked over to the graveyard, which was the topic of their consultation: their two daughters had each married eldest sons, leaving no one to inherit the family grave, so they wanted to know what they should do with it. We cannot simply abandon our ancestors, they said. They still valued their connection with Miharu, where their parents had been born, so I immediately suggested that they, too, move within our grounds.

Since I became the chief priest here, we have built a columbarium that provides space for remains and a memorial tablet, and we hold ceremonial blessings there at least once a month. I explained to the two that moving their family grave closer to Kanagawa would not guarantee its future upkeep, while on the other hand, the occasional visit to this more distant place related to their family history might lead to new discoveries. Also, relocating remains within the same grounds does not require the normal application for a permit. They apparently found these factors convincing, because they quickly agreed to that plan.

I excused myself to return to moving duties while waiting for a stoneworker to arrive, but the two remained in our living room, laughing and crying over old stories. "Such a beautiful thing, to be friends," as the poem by Mushanokōji Saneatsu (1885–1976) goes. While carrying boxes to my new home and looking at the peonies that had just bloomed

in our garden, I recalled Mushanokōji's *shikishi* paintings. Come to think of it, these peonies, too, were uprooted to make way for construction and replanted this year in a new location. Apparently, peonies are also well suited to local moves.

And there goes the doorbell again. I really need to move my computer to its new home!

65

Fish-Scale Paving

July 2019

We are now in the final stages of remodeling at our temple, and we have finally started laying paving on the grounds.

Paving at Zen temples is generally done in a style called *uroko-jiki*, or "fish-scale paving," where square tiles are laid corner-to-corner like diamonds. This is hard to walk on if the spacing does not match your stride, so a previous chief priest (namely, my father) got rid of the gaps by filling them in with side-to-side tiles. This allows you to walk without watching your feet and also suppresses weeds. While it is certainly a convenient layout, it lacks a certain tension, and because it limits the amount of exposed soil, it lowers water absorption. I therefore decided to take this opportunity to return our paving to its original form.

Walking on the restored scale paving, I found it forced me to remain clearly aware of the act of walking. Aha, I thought, it enforces *kinhin*, or "walking meditation." It is hard to think about other things while walking on this paving, so your consciousness naturally turns to walking. This must be why fish-scale paving is so popular at Zen temples.

It is possible that Kobori Enshu (1579–1647) was combining the easy-to-walk fully tiled design with this style that retains the sense of walking meditation when he developed a design in which every other stone is rotated forty-five degrees so that corners touch sides. This style is called *iroko-jiki* (*iroko* is an alternative reading of *uroko*), and it is famously used in the gardens of Konchiin at Nanzenji Temple in Kyoto. It is far easier to walk on than the point-to-point style, and the change in the stones is pleasurable, but you still must remain conscious of where you are stepping.

Looking at the restored scale paving, I found myself wanting to plant juniper moss between the stones. I have been increasing the grasses and mosses on our grounds for some time now, and last year I found a patch of juniper moss on an embankment by our cemetery that I have been keeping my eye on. We had an early start to the rainy season this year, and I was able to check online weather reports, something I don't normally do, to time the transplanting of some of that moss between rains. I found a good day to do this, one that would be followed by two days of rain, and did some replanting with the help of two parishioners. It has been a long time since I have been so happy to see rainy days, and it is truly enjoyable to watch the daily changes in a growing thing. There are dealers who sell juniper moss for quick planting, but it is much more fun to enjoy slow, natural growth.

When laying stones, we used not only granite as before, but also a volcanic rock called *emochi*, thanks to a large donation by our stone dealer. The *emochi* is four-hundred-year-old stone from a shrine in Shirakawa, cast off from the rebuilding of a stone staircase, that he had been storing on his own land because he felt it wasteful to throw away such fine old materials. That being said, he had long been looking for some way to use it, and when my wife and I expressed an interest, he said he would be thrilled if we could put it to good use.

Emochi is a soft stone that is quarried in the Emochi District of Sukagawa, Fukushima Prefecture. It is best suited to semiformal or informal contexts. We therefore used the original granite for the scale

Zen temple paving stones

Uroko-jiki
Standard
pattern

Iroko-jiki
Kobori Enshu's
design

paving of walkways, but the old *emochi* stone around a water faucet. For some reason, the contrast made me think of some territorial conflict during the Warring States period.

The Japan Coast Guard has decided to deploy three of its largest patrol boats at the Port of Kagoshima to strengthen its response to China, which has repeatedly encroached upon Japanese territorial waters around the Senkaku Islands. They also have plans for deployment to Ishigaki Island. It seems as if countries all over the world are strengthening their militaries, with the islands of the South China Sea being a particular focus of contention. I do not think there has been a period of more blatant military buildup in my lifetime.

My garden stones remind me of territorial boundaries. Of the styles, *uroko-jiki* paving stones look the most strategic, while moving from an *iroko-jiki* style to full tiling gives an increasing sense of peace and stability. I am not sure what was in the minds of those Zen monks who instructed the warlords of medieval Japan, but perhaps it is connected in some way to the illusory experience created by the four-hundred-year-old stones in our garden.

66
Scenes of the Past

August 2019

Once when I was still a monk in training at a monastery, over thirty years ago, I fell some 7 meters from the branch of a tree. Actually, it would be more accurate to say I fell along with the tree branch. Someone in the neighborhood had asked us monks-in-training to prune the branches of a chestnut tree, which we set off to do in a large group despite the fact it was raining. Apparently, an *unsui* (novice monk) who had joined us that year had been enthusiastically sawing through the branch I was standing on. I am (pretty) sure he did not do it on purpose. New arrivals were the focus of constant attention at the monastery, and were sometimes yelled at, so I suspect his nervousness resulted in tunnel vision. What I want to talk about is not his carelessness, however, but the curious experience I had while falling.

As viewed from outside, it can only have taken two or three seconds from the time I lost my balance until I hit the ground. To me, however, time seemed to be flowing in a completely different manner. I only realized later that I was experiencing what is called "life flashing before your eyes." I felt I was viewing the world as a series of black-framed images flickering from above to below in a constant stream in front of me, like film, causing me to react to each in turn. I cannot remember everything in detail, but the appearing and disappearing scenes were all significant to me. There must have been dozens of these images, and I viewed each in turn on the way to the ground.

Thankfully I landed not on my head but on the little finger of my right hand (which to this day I cannot fully extend), so my life was never in danger, despite the flipping of whatever switch it is that causes us to see those flashing images when standing at death's door. I do, however, frequently reflect on that strange experience.

Recent advances in brain research have gone far toward elucidating the mechanisms of the hippocampus, which controls our short-term memory. From what I understand, when we form new memories, new cells are generated in a mysterious part of the hippocampus called the dentate gyrus. Short-term memory is converted into long-term memory through secretion of the so-called "pleasure hormone" beta-endorphin. I wonder if "seeing your life flash before your eyes" is similar to flipping through the scrapbook of eternalized memories?

I suppose I am thinking about such things because this will be my final installment of this "*Ui no okuyama*" column, and my previous submissions, along with their lovely illustrations by Kawaguchi Sumiko, are now coming to mind. This column started in April 2012, so it has been running for nearly seven and a half years. It lasted far longer than originally planned, starting in the Home and Living section and later moving to the Culture section, and I thank those readers who stuck with me the entire time.

This column started just a year after the Tōhoku earthquake and tsunami, so at first it was hard to escape the backdrop of life in a post-disaster irradiated environment. We initiated what we called our "Great Renovations of the Heisei Era," but the former priest, my father, passed away immediately after work on our main hall was complete. After that, we started renovating the living quarters, initiating one of the busiest periods of my life, but perhaps that busyness allowed me to write about a wider variety of topics.

I named this column after a metaphor for human life in the poem "Iroha" because I figured that would allow me to write about pretty much anything I wanted. In retrospect, I feel that while the individual articles are evocative, any connections between them are strangely incidental. Perhaps life itself is merely a collection of incidentally connected events. Maybe that series of events, any causality among which is unrecognizable even to us, appears to be nothing but a "shallow dream" to others, and perhaps even we come to feel the same with the passage of time.

Ms. Kawaguchi never failed to provide us with wonderful illustrations during the run of this column, despite moving three times and becoming a mother along the way. I wonder if the many nights she spent working after getting her baby girl to bed now feel like a dream.

In any event, the past seven and a half years have without question provided me with many more scenes to flash before my eyes when the time comes, and I look forward to reviewing them at my leisure before then.

Afterword

The essays in this book originally appeared in my column "*Ui no okuyama*," which ran for approximately seven and a half years in the *Tōkyō Shimbun*, *Chūnichi Shimbun*, and *Hokuriku Chūnichi Shimbun* newspapers starting in April 2012. The first half of the series was also printed in the *Hokkaidō Shimbun* and *Nishinippon Shimbun* newspapers.

I named this column "*Ui no okuyama*," which is a metaphor for human life from the poem "Iroha," because I figured that moniker would let me write about pretty much anything I wanted. In other words, I was not planning for any kind of unified theme from the beginning, but the result was a certain choppiness that went far beyond my initial vision of the column.

My father had passed away amidst the aftermath of the Tōhoku earthquake and tsunami that had occurred the year before. Renovation work on our temple resumed immediately after that, and I was busy with many lectures, writings, and funerals. I thus constantly found myself in a state of responding to the latest sudden event.

Ui no okuyama comes from a line in "Iroha" that states: "Arriving today at the yonder side of the deep mountains of evanescent existence," which perhaps we can think of as a reference to frequently occurring unforeseen circumstances. Regardless of the plans we start out with in life, nature will always defy our expectations, leaving us to intuitively deal with situations as best we can. That is when we first realize that our speculations regarding this "evanescent existence" are themselves fetters that mislead us, in the form of "intoxication" and "shallow dreams."

The sutra that Zen priests most frequently recite, the *Daihishu Sutra*, praises the virtue of the Thousand-Armed Kannon bodhisattva. Some of my readers may be familiar with the opening of this sutra: *Namu kara tannō tora yāyā* . . . In the West, a creature with many arms and faces would almost certainly be considered a manifestation of evil, but such beings are the subjects of worship in Hindu and Buddhist cultures. This should be proof that we always emphasize the complexities of reality over Platonic idealism. In reality, it is because of the importance of inevitably dealing with nature that faith in Kannon has become widespread.

We continuously have to cope with perpetual change as we go through life, at times not knowing whether we are ascending or descending. It is similar to driving along a winding road and being unable to keep track of where we started or what altitude we are at.

In the essays presented in this book, I wrote about plants and animals, stones and wind. I wrote about my observations regarding Buddhism and Zen, nature and religion. I also described what has been going on here in Fukushima Prefecture since the earthquake, and my thoughts on architecture and soil were major recent themes. If there was a lack of consistency, it was because there was a lack of consistency in what happened to me, or in what I felt was important. I can only consider each topic as one small example of the "evanescent existence" I faced.

Just as sections accumulate into chapters and eventually become stories, people want to believe that their handling of each and every problem is another upward step toward the summit of their own deep mountains.

Zen Buddhism teaches that even in this realm of evanescent existence (*ui*), by forgetting ourselves and becoming absorbed in *yuge* (disporting oneself freely), we can slip into a different world, one of *mui*, where there is no arising or cessation. That is what it means to go to "the yonder side of the deep mountains of evanescent existence." It is entering a world in which there is no higher or lower.

We may start out with some initial expectations, but all we can really do as life moves forward is identify changes in our situations and disport ourselves freely as we live life to its fullest as it comes. That is the best way to live in the present, based on both our initial expectations and our awareness of our current situations.

This book is something like a history of how I have lived life as it came over the past eight years. As for whether I have succeeded in describing ascents up deep mountains of evanescent existence, I will leave that to my readers' judgment.

I received a great deal of help in putting together this book. I extend my particular thanks to Kawaguchi Sumiko for the many illustrations she provided for the paperback release. I always looked forward to seeing her drawings even more than reading my own completed essays. At times, I even changed what I was writing about in anticipation of the accompanying illustration. I also thank Yamahara Nozomu for the layout and design (of the Japanese edition), Nagata Shirō of Chikumashobo for his hard work in getting the book published, and Iso Chinami for her comprehensive editing services. I express my deepest gratitude for this rare opportunity to collaborate. If I asked why they did it, they would probably say they were just living life as it came. Nevertheless, directly taking on and advancing what comes to us requires grit and resolve, and it was only with their assistance that I myself was able to take on this task.

To close, I sincerely thank the four managers at *Tōkyō Shimbun* who were in charge of my column: Hosokawa Akiko, Katōgi Nobuo, Kawase Masato, and Mizuno Yasushi. From them I received extensive inspiration and support in everything from reminders of my deadlines to opinions on my compositions.

It has been a long time since I was first asked to write this column. I feel like the Harley Davidson motorcycle that was swept away from Japan in the tsunami, only to wash up on the shores of Canada. We shall see what life brings us in the years to come.

Gen'yū Sōkyū
Spring 2020

About the Author

Gen'yū Sōkyū was born in 1956 in Fukushima Prefecture. He graduated from Keio University with a major in Chinese literature, and after working in a variety of fields, he entered the training monastery for Zen monks at Tenryūji Temple in Kyoto in 1983. In 2001 he was awarded the Akutagawa Prize for his novel *Chūin no hana* (Flowers of Bardo), and in 2014 he received the Minister of Education, Culture, Sports, Science and Technology's Art Encouragement Prize for *Hikari no yama* (Mountain of Light). He is currently the chief priest of the Rinzai-school temple Fukujūji in Fukushima Prefecture. He is also a visiting professor at both Hanazono University in Kyoto and Niigata University of Pharmacy and Applied Life Sciences. After the Tōhoku earthquake and tsunami of 2011, he served on the government's reconstruction plan council and as director of the Tamakiharu Fukushima Fund, which supports young Fukushima refugees. He is the author of several novels including *Amitāba* (Amitābha), *Shikarigawa ryūkei* (A View of the Shikari River), and *Chikurin Shōja* (*Venuvana-vihāra*), as well as nonfiction books on Buddhism, Zen, and meditation, including *Gendaigoyaku Han'nyashingyō* (The Heart Sutra: A Translation into Modern Japanese), *Zenteki seikatsu* (The Zen Life), *Inochi no mama ni* (Life as It Is), and *Sōshi to asobu* (Playing with Zhuangzi).